over·the·top games

for youth ministry

cont W9-BMZ-520

Team Challenge Games

over·the·top games

for youth ministry

Group

Loveland, Colorado

Group's R.E.A.L. Guarantee to you:

This Group resource incorporates our R.E.A.L. approach to ministry—one that encourages long-term retention and life transformation. It's ministry that's:

Relational
Because learner-to-learner interaction enhances learning and builds Christian friendships.

Experiential
Because what learners experience through discussion and action sticks with them up to 9 times longer than what they simply hear or read.

Applicable
Because the aim of Christian education is to equip learners to be both hearers and doers of God's Word.

Learner-based
Because learners understand and retain more when the learning process takes into consideration how they learn best.

OVER-THE-TOP GAMES FOR YOUTH MINISTRY

Copyright © 2003 Group Publishing, Inc.

CREDITS

Contributing Authors: Steven L. Case, Mikal Keefer, Jan Kershner, Linda Klimek, Robert Klimek, Julie Meiklejohn, Julia L. Roller, and Christina Schofield
Editor: Kelli B. Trujillo
Creative Development Editor: Amy Simpson
Chief Creative Officer: Joani Schultz
Copy Editor: Dena Twinem

Book Designer and Art Director: Jean Bruns
Print Production Artist: Joyce Douglas
Illustrator: Matt Wood
Cover Art Director: Jeff A. Storm
Cover Designer: Blukazoo
Cover Photographer: Daniel Treat
Production Manager: Dodie Tipton

LIBRARY OF CONGRESS CATALOGING-IN-PUBLICATION DATA
Over-the-top games for youth ministry / [contributing authors, Steven L. Case ... et al. ; editor, Kelli B. Trujillo].
    p. cm.
    Includes index.
    ISBN 0-7644-2385-1
    1. Church group work with teenagers. 2. Games in Christian education. I. Case, Steve L., 1964- II. Trujillo, Kelli B.
    BV4447 .O79 2003
    268' .433—dc21   2002151235
10 9 8 7 6 5 4 3 2   12 11 10 09 08 07 06 05

Printed in the United States of America.
Visit our website: **www.group.com**

over·the·top games
for youth ministry

introduction

Ahhhhh...Capture the Flag. What a classic! Tons of teenagers running, hiding, laughing. Students could play it for hours! But what is it exactly that makes Capture the Flag so great? It's not just your "usual" game. It takes more than five minutes. It involves strategy, teamwork, activity, imagination. It takes place in a large space. It's over-the-top!

If you're looking for fun new games that pack that same kind of punch, *Over-the-Top Games for Youth Ministry* is the book for you. These thirty-five original games are one giant leap above your "average" youth group game. As you look through these pages, you'll find games that are *big*, involving lots of students or lots of space. You'll encounter games that take *longer* than just a few minutes and involve tons of excitement and adventure. You'll discover games that are *challenging* and will get players strategizing together and developing teamwork.

And here's the great news: There's so much variety in this book that you'll find games for any group size and any occasion. Whether you have eight students or two hundred, you'll find exciting and memorable over-the-top games that will work for you. Some make perfect short icebreakers for youth meetings while others could be the focus of an entire evening, event, or weekend retreat.

Over-the-Top Games for Youth Ministry is organized using these three categories:

- **Reality Games**—These simulations of real-life or unusual situations are guaranteed to engage your students' imaginations.
- **Group Quest Games**—During these games, players will work together to solve mysteries, decipher puzzles, or overcome challenges.
- **Team Challenge Games**—These fun activities have a team-building focus and will get teenagers working in small or large groups to accomplish a task together.

Each over-the-top game lets you know exactly what supplies you'll need, how much time the activity will take, and the estimated number of participants you'll need to make the game work. At the end of each game, you'll also find a "For Extra Impact" box that provides bonus suggestions for short discussions you can lead after the game ends.

So if you're ready to create some lifelong memories and introduce some new sure-to-be favorites, dive in for some fun that is sure to be over-the-top!

over·the·top

games

For youth ministry

reality games

Blustery Brigade

OVERVIEW: Players will work together in bucket-brigade fashion to fill buckets with water and use them to douse other teams.

TIME INVOLVED: 10 to 40 minutes

GROUP SIZE: from 10 to 100 or more participants

SUPPLIES: 1 large plastic cup per player, several plastic wading pools, at least 1 hose, one 5-gallon bucket per team

PREPARATION: This game is meant to be played outdoors. To get everything ready, set out the wading pools around the perimeter of your playing area and use the hose (or hoses) to fill them to the brim with water. Set the buckets a few feet away from each other in the center of the playing area.

Before the event, tell students to start gathering some firefighting gear to wear for the game. Their outfits can include things such as toy firefighter helmets, uniforms, boots, or suspenders. If students don't have anything that fits the theme, invite them to be creative, perhaps wearing a rain slicker, poncho, or even dressing like a Dalmatian. Also, tell students to bring a beach towel, to wear a swimsuit under their clothes, and to be prepared to get wet!

The Game

When all players have arrived dressed in their firefighter gear, have them form at least two equal-sized teams. A team should be made up of five to ten players—the more teams, the better.

Give each participant a cup, and instruct each team to line up single file behind a bucket. Each team's line should stretch in the general direction of one of the wading pools filled with water.

Explain to players that long ago, before cities had functioning fire hydrants and fancy fire engines, people used to fight fires by working together in bucket brigades. They'd form a line starting near a lake or stream and would pass bucketfuls of water from person to person all the way down the line until the water reached the burning building. The last person in the brigade

LEADER TIP

Use a hose to keep the wading pools full during the game. Just make sure only *you* get to touch the hose, otherwise players may get out of hand and spray other players or even spray you! If you have more than one hose, set the hoses in the various pools and keep them running throughout the game.

line would then throw the water onto the fire in an effort to extinguish it.

Tell teenagers that their job is to work together in their crew to move water from one of the wading pools into their bucket, using only their cups. They must do this bucket-brigade style, with the person at the end of the line filling his or her cup in the pool, dumping that water in the next person's cup, who then dumps the water in the next person's cup, and so on. The last person in line should dump his or her cupful into the team's bucket in an effort to fill it up to the top. (If teams work quickly, they can be continuously passing several cupfuls of water down their line simultaneously.)

Once a team's bucket is full, it's time to put that bucket to use. However, instead of throwing their water on a fire, they get to dump the water on one of the other fire-fighting teams. The bucket carrier can get within two feet of another team and then just splash away.

Once a bucket has been emptied, that team should begin working right away to fill it up again and keep playing.

Here are two important rules involved in the play-ing of this game. First, only the end people in each bucket-brigade line can move around, either running back and forth to a wading pool or running to the bucket. The rest of the brigade team members must pick a spot on the ground and stay there. This means

> **LEADER TIP**
>
> Encourage players to communi-cate with their team members, especially when it comes to who they decide to dump their bucket of water on. Prompt players to make it a team decision whenever possible.

that players getting doused by another brigade team cannot run away; they can only duck down or lean to the side in an effort to avoid being soaked.

Second, players are not allowed to sabotage the other teams' efforts to fill their buckets. They can't knock over each other's buckets or cups or scoop water out of each other's buckets.

In case you're wondering, the main objective of this game is just for students to have fun—and to get rather wet in the process! There's no winner or loser in this game and no set time limit. Just keep playing until it seems participants have had enough (or until their fingers begin to look like raisins).

impact

For extra...

Use this lighthearted game to discuss a heavy subject: revenge. Ask:
- *Did this game involve getting revenge? What are some examples?*
- *Did revenge feel good in this game? Why or why not?*
- *Does revenge feel good in real life?*
- *Outside of this game, have you ever wanted to get revenge on someone? What happened?*
- *Should Christians ever take revenge? Defend your answer.*

Wrap things up by inviting a student to read Romans 12:18-21 aloud. Invite teenagers to share their reaction to the Scripture passage.

Detonator

OVERVIEW: Participants will work in teams to create "detonators" that can be used to break water bombs hanging overhead.

TIME INVOLVED: 20 to 40 minutes

GROUP SIZE: from 4 to 40 participants

SUPPLIES: tricycles, water balloons, stopwatch, scissors, nails, hammer, and strong fishing line. For each tricycle, you will need a box filled with random odds and ends such as plastic bats, plastic forks, duct tape, boards, nails, a hammer, paint, brushes, a lid to a trash can, scissors, glue, twine, and so on.

PREPARATION: This activity requires warm weather and a large open playing field with trees or posts along the perimeters. Fill dozens of balloons with water. Use long pieces of fishing line to tether the water balloons together in a long string of water bombs. The length of the strings will vary depending on where the lines are to be hung. Be sure to leave long pieces of fishing line on each end to tie the string of balloons between two trees or poles about four or five feet from the ground.

To hang balloon lines, drive two small nails three-quarters of the way into the tree or pole at the appropriate height, tying one end of the water balloon line onto one of the nails. Proceed, wrapping the length of the string in a figure-eight motion several times. Then drive the nails the rest of the way into the tree or post. Follow this same procedure to hang the other end of the line onto an adjacent tree or post, pulling the line taut. Repeat these steps until you have created an aerial mine field of water bombs hanging overhead.

Locate at least two tricycles. For each tricycle you locate, prepare a box of odds and ends as described in the supplies list.

The Game

In this game, teenagers will build a detonator similar to bomb-detonating robots, except in this case, the bombs are water balloons and the robot will be a teammate on a tricycle who is equipped with whatever weaponry the team has created from the items in their box. Players will race the clock to diffuse water bombs hanging overhead. The goal of the game is for the teams to work together to detonate as many water bombs as possible.

To begin, assign students to teams. (The number of teams will depend on your group size and resources.)

Give each team a box of odds and ends and a tricycle, and invite them to get started creating their detonators. When all teams have completed their secret

LEADER TIP

If you'd like to get more students in on the action, have team members switch roles so three or four different people can ride each tricycle in the allotted time.

weapons, a volunteer from each group should show their detonator to the rest of the groups. Each team should then choose a player who will diffuse water bombs with their group's weapon while they ride around the playing field on a tricycle.

Set your stopwatch for five minutes. When you give the signal, let tricycle riders from each team go to work detonating the water balloons in the allotted time. Remind these players not to ride too close to other players or swing their weapons at anyone. If you suspect this might be a problem, let teams go one at a time for two to three minutes each. If balloons remain at the end of the game, cut them free and distribute for an all-out water war! Collect detonators afterward to prevent any accidental injuries.

impact

For extra impact

When the game has ended, say: **Sometimes life can be like a minefield, with hidden temptations waiting to hurt or destroy our walk with God.** Ask:

• **How does the devil disguise sin to make it harder to recognize?**

• **What are the weapons God has given us to combat temptation?**

• **Can you recall specific Bible verses that deal with overcoming temptation?**

• **How can we work together to defeat the devil's influence in our lives?**

If time allows, consider sharing Scripture that deals with overcoming temptation, such as 1 Peter 5:8-9 or Hebrews 10:24-25.

Diamond Smugglers

OVERVIEW: Students will act as diamond smugglers or police and simulate diamond smuggling traffic.

TIME INVOLVED: approximately 1 hour

GROUP SIZE: from 20 to 100 or more participants

> **SUPPLIES:** 30 marbles, 1 plastic bag, 2 buckets
>
> **PREPARATION:** Designate an area outside of your meeting room (such as the hallway or another room nearby) as the "smugglers' hideout." Designate a corner of your meeting room as the "police headquarters" and "jail." Place a bucket in each of these areas and put 10 marbles in the police headquarters' bucket. Fill a plastic bag with the 20 remaining marbles and put it in the smugglers' hideout.

The Game

When students arrive, divide them into two equal groups. One group will be the "diamond smugglers" and the other will be the "police." Explain that the room you're in is a traffic area for stolen "diamonds"—and all of the smuggling has been going on right under the nose of the police! The police must try to bring this smuggling to a halt and confiscate all of the stolen diamonds.

Point out the police headquarters as well as the location of the smugglers' hideout. Tell players that all of the diamond smuggling and police work must take place in the designated diamond-trafficking area. The police cannot leave the area or follow any smugglers to their hideout.

Explain the following rules to the students: As the game leader, you'll be in charge of the diamond supply—the bag of twenty marbles. What the diamond smugglers will attempt to do is move as many diamonds as they can through the trafficking area and back to their hideout. The job of the police is to try to arrest any smugglers caught with diamonds and confiscate their diamonds. There are a total of thirty diamonds in the game. The police already have ten confiscated diamonds in their headquarters and you have the other twenty. As the holder of the diamond supply, you'll be stationed just outside the entrance of the diamond trafficking area.

To smuggle a diamond, a smuggler must get one diamond from your supply and walk with it into the diamond-traffic area where other smugglers and police officers are mingling. He or she must carry the diamond in one of their hands at all times—the smuggler cannot put it in a pocket or anywhere else. Also, a smuggler can only carry one diamond at a time.

The smuggled diamond must be passed off twice before it can be brought to the smugglers' headquarters and put in their smuggled-diamonds bucket. For a diamond's first hand-off, the one passing on the diamond holds up two fingers as the diamond changes hands so that the new smuggler will know he or she is the second carrier of the diamond and it needs to be passed off again. When the second smuggler decides to pass off the diamond, he or she must hold up three fingers for the receiving smuggler. The third smuggler can then walk the diamond out of the traffic area back to the smugglers' hideout and put it in the smuggled-diamonds bucket.

Smugglers must develop their own code words or signals to communicate with each other if they'd like to pass a diamond. The smugglers should also work together to create a strategy that will confuse the police. For example, they can coordinate fake handoffs, false codes, frequently enter and exit the traffic area (with or without diamonds), or limit the number of diamonds they are smuggling at any given time.

The police are to mingle in the diamond-trafficking area and observe the smugglers as they travel in and out of the room with the goal of catching smugglers who have diamonds in their possession. Police officers can follow smugglers closely, but cannot block their way or make demands such as, "Open both of your fists!" If a police officer is suspicious that a smuggler has a diamond, the police officer can arrest that person simply by saying "You are under arrest." If the smuggler is indeed carrying a diamond, he or she must immediately turn it over to the police who will place it in their confiscated-diamonds bucket. The arrested smuggler is then taken to the police headquarters and put in jail by having to sit down and face the wall for five minutes. After five minutes, the smuggler may re-enter the game.

If a police officer wrongly arrests a smuggler who is not in possession of a diamond, the police officer must hand over a diamond from the confiscated diamonds bucket and guarantee that smuggler immediate and safe passage out of the trafficking area—the smuggler can take that diamond directly to the smugglers' hideout. For this reason, police officers should work together to make decisions about arrests, making sure to only make arrests when they have a high degree of confidence that the smuggler is in possession of the diamond.

LEADER TIP Recruit several other volunteers to help with the game. Station one at the police headquarters to help keep track of jail time, and encourage a few others to mingle in the trafficking area to ensure that the rules are being followed.

The goal of the game is for one of the teams to get all of the diamonds, so if either group notices that they have thirty diamonds in their bucket, they should declare the end of the game. It is likely, though, that this game will go on for a long time without either team coming into possession of all of the diamonds, so it is a good idea to set a time limit and call an end to the game when time is up. Invite teams to tally the number of marbles they each have and end the game by celebrating the students' teamwork.

impact

Conclude this game with a discussion about integrity. Ask:

- **How did those of you who were police officers determine if someone was smuggling a diamond?**
- **How did those of you who were smugglers attempt to cloak your actions?**
- **What are some examples in real life of people who try to hide their actions, or who try to live double lives?**
- **How would you define the word** integrity?
- **What does someone's behavior have to do with his or her integrity?**

Don't Wake Up Grandpa!

OVERVIEW: Players will try to defuse a "puzzle bomb" attached to sleeping "Grandpa's" back. The catch? They must do so without waking Grandpa or ringing any of the bells attached to Grandpa's clothing.

TIME INVOLVED: 30 minutes to 1 hour

GROUP SIZE: from 6 to 42 participants

SUPPLIES: 60 large sleigh bells, cardboard shirt box, plastic tape, duct tape, 100-piece puzzle (or a 30- to 46-piece puzzle for groups of 15 people or less), old long-sleeved shirt, needle and thread, pants, belt, sleeping cap (or baseball cap), shoes with laces, stopwatch, card table, rocking chair

PREPARATION: First select a volunteer to be "Grandpa." This is a great role for an adult leader, youth pastor, or senior pastor. This person should be big enough to cause just a little difficulty in being moved. As an added benefit, it would be great if this person were a non-ticklish, dead-weight, champion "snorer."

Next, get Grandpa dressed up by sewing ten sleigh bells to both sleeves of a shirt, from cuff to shoulder. Sew ten sleigh bells to both legs of a pair of pants for Grandpa to wear. Fasten five bells to Grandpa's belt. Fix two bells on each set of shoelaces. Put a cap on Grandpa, preferably a sleeping cap with a bell on the end (a baseball cap with a bell on top will also work).

Now empty out the puzzle into the cardboard shirt box and seal it with two small strips of tape. Firmly fasten ten sleigh bells to its top. Attach the box with duct tape to Grandpa's back with the cover side facing out. Write "Santa Bell Puzzle Bomb" on the box. Once Grandpa is ready to go, have him (or her) sit and pretend to sleep in a rocking chair in the center of your meeting room with a card table near the chair. Grandpa should be leaning back (as lightly as possible) on the puzzle box attached to the back of his or her shirt. Also make sure that Grandpa has the stopwatch or timer to use at the end of the game.

The Game

When students arrive, divide them into "bomb squad" teams of three to seven students. Gather all of the bomb squad teams together for a briefing outside of the area where Grandpa is asleep. Tell students that a crisis situation has developed and that their bomb squads will have to work together to get the situation under control before a disaster occurs.

Explain these basic facts about the "crisis situation" to your students: A 104-year-old grandfather is asleep in the next room. In his day, he was a crack super spy. He has long since retired—however, some of his old archenemies are determined to do Grandpa in as a payback for all the years he dogged them. These old adversaries have booby-trapped Grandpa in his sleep. They have placed bells on Grandpa's shoes, pants legs, belt, shirtsleeves and around the bomb box taped to his back. The bomb box is a deadly Santa Bell Puzzle Bomb. The reason it is called a Santa Bell Puzzle Bomb is because the slightest tinkling from a single sleigh bell activates its detonation sequence.

> **LEADER TIP**
> Whenever a bell makes a sound, Grandpa can add to the effect by mumbling and appearing to be about to wake up.

Explain to students that their bomb squads will take turns trying to stand Grandpa up without any bells ringing. They are not allowed to purposefully dampen any of the bells—they must move him very, very carefully. Once a squad is successful, all of the students will work together to crack the Santa Bell Puzzle Bomb code before the bomb detonates.

Determine an order for all the bomb squad teams and quietly move into the room where Grandpa is sleeping. The first bomb squad team should approach sleeping Grandpa and attempt to stand him up while Grandpa remains a dead weight. If any bell on Grandpa rings even slightly, the bomb squad must immediately stop and return Grandpa to his previous sleeping position. Once that happens, the next bomb squad can take its turn trying to stand Grandpa up.

Bomb squad teams should continue to take turns trying to stand Grandpa up until a team is successful and Grandpa is in a standing position. The team that accomplishes this task should attempt to remove and open the Santa Bell Puzzle Bomb taped to Grandpa's back without ringing any bells. If any bells *do* ring, the next squad can attempt to remove the puzzle box from standing Grandpa.

Once the puzzle box is removed and opened, it should be poured onto the table next to Grandpa's chair. Then all the squads should line up in a single file line, with squads standing together.

When Grandpa says "go!" he will start a timer that determines the amount of time the group has to assemble the puzzle, therefore deactivating the bomb. The timer can be set for any amount of time—the larger the group, the more time should be allotted, from five to up to twenty minutes.

In this relay portion of the game, one participant at a time runs up to the card table, picks up a puzzle piece, and tries to fit it into another puzzle piece. If the pieces don't match, the student should run back to the line, tag the next person, and then run to the back of the line. The next person in line can then run to the table and attempt to match two pieces together. If the pieces *do* fit, the player can continue trying to match pieces until he or she is unsuccessful.

This relay should continue until a student successfully completes the puzzle or until the time runs out and Grandpa says "BOOM!"

Once the game is done, lead the students in a round of applause for their efforts.

For extra impact

Use this game to kick-start a discussion about teamwork. Ask:
- **What is teamwork? How does teamwork work?**
- **Do teams only work best under pressure?**

• *What should teamwork look like in the church?*
• *Can a team operate if some of the members refuse to participate in what they are trying to accomplish? Explain.*

Heroes, Flying and Otherwise

OVERVIEW: Teenagers will pretend they are delegates at an international superhero convention and will guess each other's superhero identity and powers.

TIME INVOLVED: 30 minutes to 1 hour

GROUP SIZE: from 10 to 100 participants or more

SUPPLIES: index cards, envelopes large enough for the index cards (1 per participant), colored markers, paper lunch bags, mini candy bars (4 per participant), wrapped pieces of hard candy (4 per participant), pieces of bubble gum (4 per participant), large basket

PREPARATION: Fill one paper bag for each participant with four mini candy bars, four wrapped pieces of hard candy, and four pieces of bubble gum. Place these on a table near the entrance of the room along with some colored markers. Put four index cards into each envelope and set these aside.

About one week prior to the event, tell students to start thinking about new superhero identities for themselves. They should each come up with a creative name and wear a costume to the event. Encourage students, though, to keep their superhero identities a secret. Superhero names should be goofy and nonsensical, such as "Totally Aluminum Dumpster Man," "Three-Quarter-Inch Plywood Girl," "Mashed Potatoes and Gravy Boy," or "Electric Blue-Green Channel Surfer Woman."

> **LEADER TIP**
> To spice up the setting, add fantastic lighting as befits a gathering of superheroes. Use strobe lights and a mirror ball. Decorate the room in brightly colored streamers and balloons.

The Game

Hand each superhero a filled paper bag when he or she arrives, and tell each superhero that it is his or her official "Bag of Virtues." Participants can look in their bags, but can't eat anything inside until the game begins. Give each hero a chance to decorate his or her bag with colored markers. Warn participants to keep their character names secret.

Hand each hero an envelope filled with four blank index cards. Have the heroes spread out around the meeting area so they can fill out each card in private. On the first card, participants should write their superhero name.

The second card should describe their main power. This power should in some way be related to their superhero identity. These main powers can be real talents of the participants or imagined ones. Descriptions of these powers should be short and funny. An example of a main power could be "the ability to blow out five birthday candles in five breaths" or "the power to go two weeks without sleeping."

The minor-power index card should be filled out next, and should also be related to the superhero name and main power. A minor power should simply be a less impressive power, such as "the ability to tear duct tape with bare hands and handle a pair of scissors at the same time."

Finally, the fourth card should be filled out explaining the superhero's power-canceling object. This is an object that weakens the superhero (like kryptonite and Superman). This object should be logically related to the superhero's name and powers. For example, a power-canceling object for "Three-Quarter-Inch Plywood Girl" might be sandpaper.

When all four index cards are complete, have students return them to their envelopes and place the envelopes in their Bags of Virtues. Caution students again not to reveal the contents of their envelopes to anyone.

When everyone is ready, begin by welcoming students to the annual International Superheroes Convention. Tell the participants that their job is to elect a new president for the International Superhero Society. The president will be the superhero who best embodies three prime virtues: promptness, exactness, and cheerfulness. The president will be prompt, always on time for crime; exact, with single purpose of mind and heart; and cheerful, always ready to laugh in the face of danger.

Next, explain that the object of the game is for each superhero to collect the most tokens of virtue in his or her bag. Whoever has the most tokens of promptness (mini candy bars), exactness (hard candy), and cheerfulness (pieces of bubble gum) at the end of the game will become the honorary new president of the superhero society. Superheroes will acquire their tokens of virtue through guessing each other's names, powers, and power-canceling objects.

The superheroes will form pairs and take turns questioning each other during three-minute questioning rounds. At the beginning of each round, the game leader will state the topic of conversation (either the superhero's name, main power, minor power, or power-canceling object). Partners will take this time to ask each other direct yes or no questions. If, in the course of a questioning round, a superhero thinks he or she knows the contents of one of his or her partner's index cards, the questioning superhero can take a guess. If the guess is basically correct, the proper index card from the questioned superhero's envelope must be surrendered to the other superhero. (The superhero who has been guessed can no longer be questioned by other superheroes on that topic.) The superhero who guessed correctly also gets to take a token of virtue (any kind he or she wants) from the other superhero's Bag of Virtues. This newly acquired virtue should be added to the guesser's Bag of Virtues. However, if the guess is wrong, the questioned superhero gets to take a token of virtue from the questioner's Bag of Virtues.

At the end of each three-minute round, the game leader will instruct superheroes to switch partners. If no guess is made by either partner before time is up in a round, both players are to take a single virtue token from their bags and immediately consume it. (Tokens of cheerfulness (bubble gum) need to stay in player's mouths the entire duration of the game, though they can *temporarily* remove their gum in order to consume their other treats.)

If a superhero runs out of virtue tokens, he or she automatically becomes a sidekick to the superhero to whom he or she lost his or her final token of virtue. As a sidekick, this superhero becomes a living and breathing "Free Turn Token" for the winning superhero. The winning superhero can use his or her sidekick if he or she makes a wrong guess during a questioning round or runs out of tokens of virtue. If this occurs, the superhero can surrender the sidekick to the questioning superhero instead of surrendering a token of virtue. While a sidekick is with a superhero, the sidekick should try to help him or her during the questioning and guessing process.

Ask the students if they have any questions about the rules you've explained. Once you've answered their questions, begin the game!

Three-minute questioning rounds should proceed from one topic to the next (superhero name, main power, minor power, and power-canceling object). Round topics can be repeated in this order several times. Keep a close watch on the progress of the game. Once you feel enough people have run out of their tokens or have eaten a good portion of them, a count up should be called.

Have all of the students count up their tokens for each of the three virtues. The superhero who has the most tokens in all or two out of three categories of virtues becomes the new president of the superhero society. (If there is a tie, then make both superheroes honorary presidents.) The president's first act as the new leader should be to put all the remaining tokens in a large basket, gather all the super-heroes around, and then fling all the candy into the air for everyone to share.

End the game by having students mingle about as they eat their candy, revealing their superhero identities, powers, and power-canceling objects to each other. (If your group is small enough and you have enough time, invite players to take turns sharing their identities, powers, and power-canceling objects with the entire group.)

For extra impact

Use this game to begin a discussion about real-life heroes. Ask:
- ***What does it mean to be a hero?***
- ***What should heroes act like?***
- ***Name a hero you have actually met. What virtues does your hero possess?***

Missionary Boot Camp

OVERVIEW: Teenagers will get a taste of some of the adventures and challenges missionaries encounter as they minister in unique settings.

TIME INVOLVED: 1 to 2 hours (depending on group size)

GROUP SIZE: from 4 to 42 participants

SUPPLIES: signs marking all stations by number and name (for example, Station 1: Traveling Light), whistle, photocopy of "Station Descriptions" (pp. 24-27). You'll also need the following supplies for each station.

1. *TRAVELING LIGHT STATION:* suitcase; 1 sheet of paper and pen for each group; at least 10 potential packing items, such as an empty pill box marked malaria pills, bug spray, sleeping bag, mosquito net, Bible, bottled

water, biscuit mix, frying pan, portable CD player, towel, coat, swimsuit, pants, shirt, and so on.

2. *WELCOME FEAST STATION:* beef jerky strips, potato chips, chocolate-covered raisins, bandannas, paper towels, table, chairs.

3. *WELCOME DANCE STATION:* body paint or other decorations, pole (could be a large piece of wood, the handle of a large broom or shovel, or something else), table, hand mirrors.

4. *MAGIC WATER STATION:* water basin filled with water.

5. *CHRISTIAN MUSIC? STATION:* CD player and previewed secular CD that mentions God (such as albums by DMX, Creed, Lifehouse, or a group a student recommends).

6. *RESURRECTION STATION:* chair

PREPARATION: Review the "Station Descriptions" handouts (pp. 24-27) to get a general idea of what will take place at each station during this game. Then find volunteers to help you run the stations. We recommend one to two volunteers for each station, except the Resurrection station which requires only one volunteer. One man and at least two women (or one woman and at least two men) are needed for the Magic Water station. Photocopy the "Station Descriptions" handouts (pp. 24-27) and cut them apart, giving each volunteer group the copy of their station's instructions.

> **LEADER TIP**
> Assign the stations to your volunteers a week or so before you play the game, and give them a copy of the instructions and scripts for their stations so that they can be better prepared to answer questions and can help organize the supplies and setup.

Prepare six rooms or stations with enough space in between them that the students won't be distracted by what is going on at the other stations. Some or all of the stations can be outside if weather permits. Mark each station with a clearly labeled sign so the groups can move easily between them. For the first station, Traveling Light, set up an open suitcase and scatter the potential packing items around the room. For the second station, Welcome Feast, get a table long enough for all the students in one group to sit at and

> **LEADER TIP**
> If you have a small youth group and they can go through the stations as one or two groups, then you can go with fewer volunteers. Just give volunteers double duty by assigning them more than one station.

place chairs around it. Break up the beef jerky into small enough pieces so that each teenager can have one. Place a paper towel over the food or hide it so that the students will not see it.

For the third station, Welcome Dance, you'll need to set up a pole in the center of the station area and a table for the face paints and hand mirrors. The fourth station, Magic Water, just requires a place for one male volunteer and his "wives" to sit and something on which to place the water basin filled with water. For the fifth station, Christian Music?, you'll need to set up the CD player and CD you selected. The last station, Resurrection, will only require a place for a volunteer to sit.

The Game

Say: **In a few weeks, your team is going to be dropped off on a remote Pacific island as a missionary team from our church. We've developed this camp to help you get ready for the challenge. We like to call it Missionary Boot Camp.**

Have participants form groups of about four to seven students. (If you have less than eight students, simply have them all work together as one group.) Send Group 1 to the first station, Traveling Light. If you just have a few groups, it would be best to have the other groups wait and listen to music or talk so they can go through the stations in order. However, if you have more than three groups, you may want to start them all at the same time with the stations that correspond to their group numbers.

Your job will be to monitor the stations and keep time so that each group rotates from station to station without finishing too early or not having enough time. Allow about seven to ten minutes for each station, and use the whistle when it's time to switch. Direct groups to rotate to the next station each time you blow your whistle.

For extra impact

Once every group has finished each station, have your students pair up with students who weren't in their original group to discuss these questions. Ask:
* *What items did you pick to take with you? Why did you choose those?*
* *How did you feel about eating strange food? What would you say if one of the cooks had asked if they could use yak meat for communion?*

- *What did you decide about participating in the Welcome Dance? baptizing a polygamist and his wives? listening to the music? Explain your decisions.*
- *Has your experience changed your ideas of what it means to be a missionary?*
- *How did it feel to have someone ask you what the resurrection means? Do you feel that you explained it well?*

Conclude by having the groups gather back together and share their insights.

station descriptions

(Station 1: Traveling Light appears on p. 27.)

STATION 2: *Welcome Feast*

When students arrive at your station, say: **Welcome to our island! We have prepared a welcome feast for you with our very own specialties. It means a lot to us that you share in this tradition with us. It is customary for guests to be blindfolded when they eat here. That way they can savor the good food without anything to distract them from their taste buds.**

Place a bandanna over each teenager's eyes, then say: **The first course is cow patty chips.** Place a potato chip in each teenager's mouth. **Cows are sacred animals here, so we value *everything* that comes from them.**

Ask: • **Is anyone here a vegetarian?** (If there are vegetarians, give them potato chips for the next course as well.)

Say: **Our special entree is dried yak meat, a real delicacy.** Place a small piece of beef jerky in each participant's mouth.

Say: **Dessert is cocoa beans and cockroaches. It's very good and has lots of protein. Unfortunately, the chocolate takes away some of the tasty crunchiness of the roaches.** Place a chocolate-covered raisin in each teenager's mouth.

Station 3: *Welcome Dance*

In this station, you will be preparing for a celebration similar to the Native American Sun Dance. All volunteers should be dressed in costume using face paint, a headdress, feathers, or other decorations.

When participants arrive at your station, say: **We have a special ceremony to welcome you and I think you Christians will like it very much. The purpose of the ceremony is to bless the community. We dance around this pole for four days as a way of praying that our god will be with us throughout your visit. Use the paints to decorate your faces and arms for the dance. It is customary for someone else to do your face paint.**

After the teenagers have painted themselves (be careful with time here—only allow five or fewer minutes for painting), say: **In this welcome dance, each of us will be pierced through the chest with a bone skewer. The pain represents the suffering that we take on for the community, much like the pain Jesus suffered on the cross. We believe, however, that we need to do the suffering rather than Jesus. Will you participate in this ceremony with us? It would mean a lot to our community—a real sign that you have solidarity with us.**

Another volunteer should then say: **You can take the rest of the time to discuss whether or not you would take part in this ceremony. Come to a decision, and be prepared to defend it. You may want to consider these questions: Is the welcome dance like Christianity? Could the welcome dance be viewed as an expression of Christianity? Would participating in the dance be against your Christian beliefs? Is it more important to learn local customs or to teach about Christianity as you know it? You can ask any questions of me that you would like.**

Be prepared to answer any questions as participants make their decision.

Station 4: *Magic Water*

One member of your volunteer group will act as a polygamist while the other members should serve as spouses.

When students arrive at your station, the polygamist volunteer should say: **I have heard about this Jesus and the baptism trick. I have decided to become baptized, and I have told each of my five wives [husbands] that they will also be baptized. They're not too excited about it, but they'll do what I say. We brought the water with us, so can you go ahead and baptize us right now? It's OK to still practice our local religion, right? Either way, we want to receive the Christian magic as soon as possible.**

You must decide whether you would baptize me and my wives [husbands]. **You can ask us any questions that you want.**

If asked, the spouses should say that they know nothing about baptism and are only obeying their husband [wife]. If the students are running out of questions or seem confused, prompt them with further comments about your native religion or questions about what baptism means.

Station 5: *Christian Music?*

Blast music from the prepared CD, and dance around when students arrive at your station. Once they're all seated, say: **We're so glad to see you. I hope that you have brought more of this Christian music. It talks about God, and I have created a dance to the music that I would like to perform at our first church service.**

Demonstrate the dance; make it as silly or as serious as you like. Then say: **Your task is to decide whether it would be appropriate to participate in this song and dance. If so, why and with what limitations? If not, what could you perform in its place?**

Encourage the members of the group to talk about what secular music that refers to religious themes means in their lives and what image of Christianity it might present to non-Christians.

Station 6: *Resurrection*

As students arrive at your station, sit in a chair in the center of the room. Say: **I am glad you have come because I am very confused. I do not understand exactly what this "resurrection" is and what it means for me. Can you tell me why it matters in my life?**

Ask the group members to try to answer your question, and ask them questions that a non-Christian might ask.

Station 1: *Traveling Light*

When students enter the room, say: **Welcome to Missionary Boot Camp. There are serious weight restrictions on the prop plane you will be taking to the island, so you'll have to make some decisions about what is most important to take with you. We've provided some items for you to choose from, but you can only take seven of them. You have to work together to choose the seven items you will take, and you only have a few minutes, so get started. Once you have finished your selections, write them down, and we'll discuss them later with the other groups.**

Observe students as they make their decisions, but don't offer any help.

Mrs. Taft's Hat

OVERVIEW: Teenagers will pretend to be a team of security guards at the Museum of National History that has just been hit by an earthquake. They will work together to remove the historical treasures from the building.

TIME INVOLVED: approximately 30 minutes

GROUP SIZE: from 10 to 50 participants

SUPPLIES: blindfolds; earplugs, headphones, or earmuffs; bandage tape; wheelchair or crutches; fabric for slings; knee braces. You'll also need 1 museum item for every student in your group. These items should range in size from a safety pin to a sofa and should be labeled to identify their historical significance. Use this list for ideas to get started: plastic hoops ("practice rings for WWII bomber pilots"), butcher paper ("the original Constitution"), light bulb ("Edison's first"), sofa ("from Kennedy living quarters"), dining room chair ("from Washington's first office"), safety pin ("brooch worn by Mrs. Roosevelt at the inauguration"), desk ("first desk in oval office"), brick ("from the foundation of the Washington Monument"), Frisbee disc ("steering wheel from Henry Ford's first car"), hat ("from the collection of Mrs. William Howard Taft"), pair of rubber kitchen gloves ("Teddy Roosevelt's riding gloves"), bicycle ("from the shop of Orville and Wilbur Wright"), or orange parking lot cone ("megaphone used by George W. Bush in college cheerleading days"). If you're in a country other than the United States, modify labels to fit your country's national history.

PREPARATION: If you're playing this game outside, use a large open area. Designate several different spots where various museum items are stacked. For an indoor version of the game, place groups of items in different rooms. Create a simple map for participants that lists the items and where they can be found.

The Game

Begin by reading this scenario: **You are a team of highly trained security guards at the Museum of National History. Suddenly, without warning, a large earthquake has just rocked the city. All of you have been injured in some way by falling debris. The structure of the building is unstable, and you've just learned that any** aftershocks may cause the entire building to collapse and destroy the national treasures inside. Despite the threat to your safety, you've decided to work together as a team to remove as many of the historical treasures as possible before the next aftershock.

Next, use the earplugs, blindfolds, bandages, crutches, and other first-aid supplies to "injure" the participants. Select some who will be deafened, others who will be blinded, and several who will be bandaged on arms, hands, or legs. Clarify that any body part that is bandaged is severely hurt and cannot be used during the game.

Explain to participants that the object of the game is for players to work together to get all the items from their current location back to the starting line. The group must work together in order to achieve this feat. The extra challenge is that every student must cross the finish line with one of the museum items. Obviously, individual students won't be able to move the large objects alone, so objects can also be combined. For example, a student can pin a safety pin to his or her shirt and help someone else carry a desk.

Remind participants that this is not a competition or a timed game. The game is over when all of the team members have crossed the finish line and accomplished the goal together.

impact

for extra

Say: A lot of the "injuries" you were given caused you to do things the way some people have to live every day. Imagine what your life would be like if these injuries were permanent. Ask:

- What was most challenging to you about functioning with your injury?
- How did you rely on other people?
- Did you get the help you needed? Why or why not?
- Do you have any disabilities in real life, such as a sight problem that requires glasses, a chronic illness, or a more serious physical problem? How does it affect your daily living?
- How can you show greater compassion and kindness to people dealing with serious physical ailments or challenges?

Relic Hunters

OVERVIEW: In this game based on the period of Roman persecution of Christians, participants will work together to overcome challenges and evade "Roman soldiers" in order to recover "sacred Christian objects" hidden in the woods.

TIME INVOLVED: 2 to 3 hours

GROUP SIZE: from 10 to 50 or more participants

SUPPLIES: several "relics" such as crosses, a communion cup (chalice), a communion plate, a fish symbol, or Bibles; masking tape; plastic boxes; squirt guns; 3 prepared envelopes for every 5 students; clipboard with paper and pen; first-aid kit

PREPARATION: This game should take place in a large outdoor area where participants can find cover easily. A forested area with a central meeting point or adjacent parking lot would work best. Hide the "relics" in large plastic boxes in locations you select. (To figure out the number of relics you need, divide the number of participants by five. For example, if you expect to have about twenty students, hide four relics.) It's a good idea to hide the relics immediately before the game to minimize the risk of a person or animal moving them. You may also want to secure them with bungee cords if you hide them in a tree, or mark the spot with something if you bury them.

Assess the layout of the playing area and establish some boundaries that you'll communicate to students. Set aside a small section of the playing area that will be a "jail."

You'll also need to prepare three sealed envelopes for each group of participants to open, one each hour in succession, with the following instructions.

Envelope 1: Create a clue that will help the group find their relic, but not one that will give it away too soon. For example, you could write "Your relic is the chalice. It is located above the ground near a very large oak by the head of a trail."

Envelope 2: Write a challenge that team members will have to deal with. For example, you could write "One of your team members has broken his or her leg. That person will now have to be carried or supported every time you move or hide."

Envelope 3: Create a final challenge that will impede communication. For example, you could write, "A high concentration of soldiers in the area has made talking an extreme liability. You must now communicate with hand signals to avoid detection."

For this game, you'll need to recruit several adult volunteers who will participate in the game as Roman soldiers. Ideally, you should have one to three adult volunteers per team of players. If, for example, you had ten teams (with five students each), you should try to have ten to thirty adult volunteers.

> **LEADER TIP**
>
> This would be a great game to play during a Saturday afternoon of a weekend retreat.

Before game day, tell students and adult volunteers to wear watches and dress in camouflage-colored clothes that they can get dirty. If it will be a hot day, you may also want to remind them to bring canteens or water bottles.

The Game

Begin the game by saying: **Starting in A.D. 64 during the rule of Nero and continuing until the reign of Constantine, Christians living in the Roman empire were persecuted for practicing their faith. They had to meet in secret, in places like catacombs, and hide their symbols and sacred objects to avoid being discovered and killed by Roman soldiers. Christians even marked their houses with the fish symbol, which meant "Jesus Christ, Son of God, Savior," so they would know one another.**

Today you are going to become persecuted Christians in search of the relics that have been left by fallen brothers and sisters. Since the people who left those relics are dead or imprisoned, you aren't exactly sure where the objects are, and the clues are vaguely written so the precious items won't be discovered by soldiers if the notes are intercepted. You're going to divide into teams and each team will be responsible for finding one of the relics.

Take your teenagers to the meeting point you have predetermined. Say: **This is our meeting place. If any of you needs help or if anyone on your team is hurt, come back here immediately. An adult will stay here at all times during the game. Also come back to this spot if you complete your task, and you will be assigned a new task.**

Divide the students into groups—one group per hidden relic. The game works best with teams of four to five participants. Advise them that teams can join forces if they wish, but it probably wouldn't be advantageous for two reasons: (1) The soldiers are more likely to find them if they move in larger groups, and (2) each group has a different relic to find. Hand them the masking tape and instruct them to mark themselves as Christians with fish symbols on the backs of their shirts.

Say: **The rest of the adults are going to be Roman soldiers, so you need to be constantly alert. Any Roman soldier will be marked by a masking-tape X on the front and back of his or her shirt. If a soldier sees you and shoots you with a water gun, you will be taken to the prison.**

Explain where the jail is located and clarify that the jail will be guarded by soldiers.

Say: **It will then become another responsibility of your team to rescue any fallen comrades from the prison. So even if you find your relic, you still need to work to rescue any captured teammates before you have finished the game. You can rescue a teammate simply by touching him or her, but if a soldier shoots you with a water gun, you will join that person in prison. Be careful because the prison will be guarded by soldiers!**

Have participants synchronize their watches, and let them know when the game will end, in two or three hours. Clarify that all students should return to the starting point at the set time, whether they've completed the challenge or not.

Pass out the envelopes to each team and say: **You are now getting three numbered envelopes. Open the first when you get into the woods and pick out a home base. It will tell you which relic you are looking for and give you some hints as to where to find it. If you find another relic, please put it back where you found it, and don't tell any other teams. The other envelopes are to be opened each hour. After one hour of play, open the second. After two hours of play, open the third. You must follow the directions in the envelope to remain in the game.**

LEADER TIP

If you'd like the game to be shorter than three hours, simply adjust the increments in which you'd like students to open envelopes. If they open them every forty-five minutes, the game will last about two hours. If they open them every thirty minutes, the game will last about an hour and a half.

Instruct the adult volunteers that they should go on patrol around the playing area for a few minutes every fifteen minutes to half an hour, but should not spend the entire game in the forest. Leave it up to their discretion if they want to guard the prison the entire game or not. Ask them to be aware of how many students they have captured. If they're not catching anyone, they should increase their patrols. If half of the participants are in prison, have them take a break from patrolling and relax their prison guard duty a little. Make sure they have the masking-tape X's on their shirts so that they are easily identifiable.

If players finish the challenge and come back early, give them a few options. They can go back as soldiers once you tape their shirts (if you have extra water guns) or they can return to try to help another team. Use your clipboard to keep track of who is joining each team so things don't become too uneven. If there are too many soldiers, the other teams won't be able to play well.

impact

Gather your students together for a discussion. Ask:

- **Were you successful in finding your relics? What challenges did you face along the way?**
- **What do you think it was like for the early Christians to have to hide their faith from the government?**
- **Do you think you would have remained true to Christian beliefs if you had faced this kind of persecution? Why or why not?**
- **How does it make you feel to know that many Christians in the world today face similar persecution and risk their lives to believe in Christ?**

for extra

Runaway Train

OVERVIEW: Players will work in runaway train teams to create crazy train tracks for them to travel on as they try to cross a large playing field.

TIME INVOLVED: 30 minutes to 1 hour

GROUP SIZE: from 20 to 100 or more participants

SUPPLIES: measuring cup, 2 orange parking lot cones, 3 cups of pebble-grade gravel per team, 3 cups of mulch per team, 3 cups of large-grade gravel per team, 15 soda cans per team, 3 pieces of lumber per team, 15 sheets of newspaper per team, 5 large garbage bags per team, 5 paper grocery bags per team, 5 plastic grocery bags per team, 1 roll of toilet paper per team, 1 bucket of plastic-foam packing peanuts per team, 3 large resealable plastic bags per team

PREPARATION: Select a very large playing area—an empty parking lot is best. Measure out the indicated amounts of gravel and mulch, and put them in individual plastic bags. Next, divide up all of the supplies into equal piles for each team, placing the piles side by side at one end of the playing field. The piles should be organized in a row for each team, with the supplies placed in the following order using the amounts specified in the Supplies list on page 33: pebble-grade gravel, large garbage bags, large-grade gravel, soda cans, various-sized lumber, newspaper, paper grocery bags, toilet paper, plastic grocery bags, plastic foam packing peanuts, and mulch.

At an opposite end of the playing area, set out two orange parking lot cones to mark the finish line.

LEADER TIP

Have your church family help out by donating the items indicated in the supply list. Some of these supplies can come from recycling bins in family homes. Some items, like the pebble- and large-grade gravel, can come from back yards or can be purchased inexpensively at a hardware and garden supply store.

The Game

When students arrive, divide them into teams of ten to fifteen students. Set the scene by telling students to imagine that each team is a different railroad company back in the days when trains were the newest form of transportation. Each of their companies is pioneering a new railway line across rugged terrain, and their goal is to successfully build their train tracks and get their train across without being derailed or stopped by obstacles.

Next, explain to players that each team will attempt to create a crazy rail line from their supply pile to the indicated finish line at the other end of the playing area. To do this, each team will form a snakelike single-file line and will stay in this order and formation until they reach the finish line.

To build their track, the first player on a team picks up the first supply item (pebble-grade gravel) and pours it in a narrow line in front of him or her. This player now walks over this "track" of gravel, being careful to walk only on the gravel, not on the parking lot surface. Then the next player in line picks up the next indicated item (garbage bags). This student can step off the track only to get around the previous team member and lay the bags lengthwise, end-to-end, in front of him or her. That player then walks over the bags to the end of the track, as does the previous player (in a single-file train line).

This process of laying out items from the supply pile and walking over them in a "train line" continues as the team proceeds toward the finish line.

One important rule is that only the current track-building student is allowed to step off the track in order to move around the rest of the students—everyone else must step only on the track surface. Once the track-building student has laid out his or her supplies, he or she must once again walk only on the track.

When all of the students have laid out a supply, if there are still items left, the last person in line (formerly the very first person) should walk backwards over the track material, pick up the next supply item, walk around to the head of the team line and lay out the new item.

Once a team has used up all of its supply items, players need to collect and pass forward the last item in their track to the front of the train for reuse. In the case of loose materials, such as the pebble gravel, these items should be collected back in their plastic bags, passed forward to the front of the train, and then poured back out on the pavement to form another track link. Tell students that every time a team pours out a loose object, it is a good idea to leave the container next to the objects for reuse, such as leaving the bucket next to the packing peanuts. Each team should continue this track-building process until its train line has been completed and they have successfully arrived at the finish line.

There is one twist to the game, however: The various railway companies can attempt to block other rail lines by speedily building their tracks across the path of an oncoming team. No team may cross over or knock aside another team's tracks. If a team's line is blocked, they have two options. They can attempt to quickly build around the front of the blocking line. Or they can attempt to move around the back of this blocking rail line as the other team moves their track forward.

When you're done explaining these directions, ask participants if they have any questions about the game. When all the students and supplies are ready, start the game!

As teams complete the challenge of building a crazy set of tracks to the finish line, they should cheer on any remaining teams.

For extra impact

Use this game to begin a discussion about the paths people follow in their lives. Ask:

• **How does it feel to build something from scratch? How is that like building**

paths for our lives?
* *What happens when you run into obstacles along the way?*
* *What role does God play in the direction of your life path?*

Rush Hour

OVERVIEW: Teenagers will work together to exchange places in a line so that everyone is facing the same direction.

TIME INVOLVED: 15 to 45 minutes (depending on group size)

GROUP SIZE: from 6 to 20 participants

SUPPLIES: paper plates, marker, tape

PREPARATION: Using the illustration below as a guide, draw one arrow on each paper plate (be sure to save a blank plate for the middle of the line). You'll need one arrowed plate for each person in your group. Set the plates out as shown, with about one foot between plates. Tape the plates to the floor.

The Game

Begin the game by having each participant stand on one of the arrowed paper plates, facing the direction indicated by their arrow. Say: **Wow! It looks like you've been caught in rush hour! Here's what you'll need to do. See how your plates have arrows pointing one direction or the other? Your job is to move everyone in the direction of the arrows so that when you're finished, the people who are now standing on the left side will be standing in the same order on the right side and the people who are now on the right side will be standing in the same order on the left side. You will always face the direction you are facing now.**

Here are the rules: You can move into an empty space in front of you, and you

can move around a person who is facing you into an empty space. You can also move one step backward into an empty space behind you. However, you can't move around anyone who is facing the same direction you are (whose back is to you), and you can't make any move that involves more than one person changing spots at the same time. Are there any questions?

If participants get really stuck, you may want to review the rules with them again. Emphasize parts of the rules that may apply to their current situation. If this doesn't help, you may want to suggest one move a person can make. Usually, once one good move has been made, participants can see their way to the solution.

L
E
A
D
E
R

T
I
P

Answer any questions students may have and then begin the game. As group members work together to decide on a strategy and begin to move, circulate around the group, offering encouragement and reinforcement of the rules. Try not to offer suggestions, even if students ask for them. It's best if players can figure out a solution on their own.

When the group has solved the problem, ask them to return to their original places and do it again, this time explaining their moves one at a time.

If you or your students are baffled, here's one sample solution to this challenge.

Based on the diagram above, student E could first step forward into the blank space. Student D could jump around student E into the new blank space. Student E could then step forward again into the blank space. Next student C could jump around student E into the blank space. Student E could then move forward into the blank space. Student B could jump around student E into the blank space. Student E could then move forward into the blank space. Next student A could jump around student E into the blank space. Finally, student E could move forward into the blank space. This pattern of steps will have successfully moved student E to the other end of the line.

After this is accomplished, students A, B, C, and D could all take one step backward, thus moving the blank space in between student D and student F. The pattern described above could then be repeated, moving student F all the way down the line until student F is next to student E. Again, students A, B, C, and D could shift backward one step and continue the process until the students have successfully switched spots.

impact

After the group has solved the puzzle, Ask:
- *What made your strategy successful?*
- *Did the group follow just one person's lead or many people? How did you decide who to follow?*
- *What was it like to follow? to lead?*
- *How did working together help you solve this challenge?*
- *How can others help you overcome real-life challenges?*

Virtues and Vices

OVERVIEW: Participants will play a card game that represents developing virtues and rejecting vices in everyday life situations.

TIME INVOLVED: 15 minutes to 1 hour

GROUP SIZE: from 4 to 100 or more participants

SUPPLIES: for each group of 4 students: 1 deck of playing cards, 1 serving platter, 1 small cardboard box, 1 photocopy of "Virtues and Vices Key" (p. 40)

PREPARATION: Make enough photocopies of the "Virtues and Vices Key" (p. 40) so that every group of four students can have one. Place a serving platter, a deck of cards, and a cardboard box in each playing area.

The Game

Invite participants to form groups of four. Each group should place its cards on the serving platter—this pile is called the "Pile-O-Life." The cardboard box will serve as a discard container.

Explain the following rules to the students. To begin the game, each player draws five cards from the Pile-O-Life. As indicated on the "Virtues and Vices Key," spades represent faults, clubs represent failings, hearts represent virtues, and diamonds represent blessings.

Play begins when a player draws a single new card from the Pile-O-Life. The player must show this card to the other three players before playing it. If the card is a virtue (heart) or blessing (diamond), the player puts the card in his or her hand. If the card is a fault (spade) or a failing (club), the player places the card faceup on the table.

To beat that card, so that it stays out of the player's hand and can be discarded, the player must name a specific example of the fault or failing assigned to the card. (These examples can be real situations from their own lives or can be made-up situations.) For example, if the card is a nine of clubs, the example may be a teenager being rude to his mother because he is frustrated with her.

Next, the player must pull from his or her hand a virtue or blessing card of equal or higher value and state specifically how that virtue or blessing would defeat the fault or failing. For example, the player may play a king of diamonds and explain that by choosing to be patient instead of frustrated and rude, the teenager could avoid hurting his mom's feelings. The virtue or blessing card that is played should be placed in the cardboard box with the fault or failing card.

If the player is unable to play an equal or higher virtue or blessing card, the player must retain the fault or failing card and add it to his or her hand.

At the completion of each turn, if no one objects to the reasoning given by the current player, the game proceeds to the next person (clockwise). If someone rejects the description given as not specific enough or unrealistic, the player must retain that fault or failing card for the rest of the game.

When the Pile-O-Life runs out, the game ends and students should tally their points according to the following point values: numbered cards are worth their numerical value, jacks are worth 11, queens are worth 12, kings are worth 13 and aces are worth 14. Virtue and blessing card values should be added while vice and failing card values should be subtracted from the total points. Final scores may be negative or positive.

If a player runs out of cards during the play of the game, the hand stops immediately. The player is awarded an automatic 50 points while the other students add the values of their cards.

Encourage students to play several rounds and keep a running score through a series of hands. Afterward, invite the student with the highest score in each group to lead a discussion with the other students about how the choices in the game can be applied to real life.

Virtues and Vices Key

HEARTS	VIRTUES
Ace	Love
King	Faith
Queen	Hope
Jack	Fortitude
10	Chastity (Purity)
9	Holiness
8	Humility
7	Forgiveness
6	Wisdom
5	Patience
4	Service
3	Healing
2	Laughter/Humor

DIAMONDS	BLESSINGS
Ace	Friendship
King	Patience
Queen	Kindness
Jack	Calmness
10	Peacefulness
9	Respectfulness
8	Perseverance
7	Courage
6	Truthfulness
5	Contentment
4	Encouragement
3	Gentleness
2	Compassion

SPADES	FAULTS
Ace	Hate
King	Untrustworthiness
Queen	Despair
Jack	Weakness
10	Impurity
9	Worldliness
8	Pride
7	Revenge
6	Arrogance
5	Uncaring
4	Selfishness
3	Hurtfulness
2	Cruelty

CLUBS	FAILINGS
Ace	Loneliness
King	Self-centeredness
Queen	Spitefulness
Jack	Anger
10	Over-indulgence
9	Rudeness
8	Laziness
7	Cowardice
6	Lying
5	Envy
4	Insulting
3	Crudeness
2	Unforgiving

For extra impact

Use this game as a natural transition into a discussion about dealing with our own faults and failings. Ask:

• *How can our faults and failings dig us into a hole? Explain.*

• *How can living out virtues affect your everyday life? Give examples.*

• *How have other people's actions and attitudes been a blessing to you?*

Volcano!

OVERVIEW: Participants will prepare for an imminent "natural disaster."

TIME INVOLVED: 30 minutes to 1 hour (depending on group size)

GROUP SIZE: from 10 to 50 participants

SUPPLIES: masking tape, photocopies of "The Big Boom!" (p. 44), scissors, one die, index cards, pens

PREPARATION: Use masking tape to create a huge game board of grid lines on the floor with a big island in the middle and a smaller island in each corner (see illustration on page 42). The middle island should be big enough for all the players to stand on. Make several photocopies of the "The Big Boom!" handout (p. 44), and cut apart the cards. Find the erupting volcano cards and take them out. Shuffle the cards, and then put one volcano card back in toward the bottom of the deck.

The Game

Begin by giving each student five index cards and a pen. Ask students to think of their most prized possessions and write them down, one item per card.

Have students stand on the large island in the middle of the game board. Say: **You've all been vacationing on the island of Wooloba. You've had a great time playing in the sand, surfing, getting a killer tan, and eating amazing food. But there's something your travel agent didn't tell you...the island of Wooloba is**

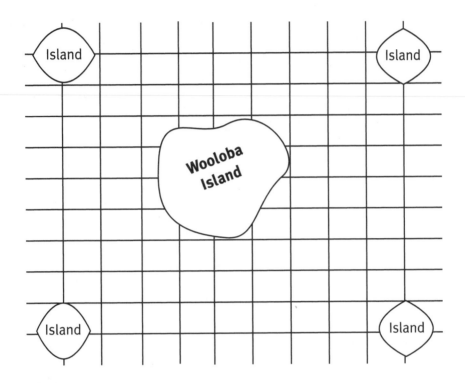

sitting right on top of an active volcano. It only erupts every one hundred years, and guess how long it's been since the last eruption? Ninety-nine years, 364 days. You need to get off the island—right now!

Explain to students that they'll be taking turns as they move off of the island to the smaller islands surrounding Wooloba. Say: **On each turn, you will first roll the die. Then you have a few choices. You can use all of your roll to move toward a safe island—one number equals one space, so if you roll a three, you'll get to move three spaces. Or you can use some of your roll to take your possessions with you—one number equals one item you can carry with you. The cards you wrote on earlier represent the items you have on the island. Every item you don't get off of the island will be lost forever. Or, you may choose to "donate" some or all of your roll to a friend to help him or her get off the island to safety. It's up to you, and you can do any combination of these things each time you roll the die.**

LEADER TIP

To add to the "island vacation" effect, you may want to have students come dressed in Hawaiian-print shirts, shorts, and flip-flops. Decorate the room with palm fronds and leis.

Explain that after a student has moved, he or she will draw a card. These cards can be good things or bad things. For example, some cards have boats on them. If a player draws a boat, he or she can use the boat to double every roll on upcoming turns. But some of the cards have things such as whirlpools or sharks on them that penalize players in some way. And one of the cards has a picture of a volcano erupting—when someone draws that card, the game is over.

Check and see if players have any questions, then begin the game. Have students take turns rolling the die and moving and drawing a card. Use the key at the bottom of the "The Big Boom!" handout to explain what the cards mean. When a person reaches one of the smaller islands, he or she will still roll the die and draw a card during each turn. He or she can decide to use the roll to bring his or her possessions or to help other people by placing the card somewhere on the grid. That way, a person who lands on that spot will automatically receive that card.

When a player draws the erupting volcano card, the game has ended. Shout out "Boom!" and then congratulate players on their efforts.

for extra impact

When the volcano has erupted, have students sit down and discuss the following questions. Ask:

• *How far did you get in the game? How do you feel about your progress?*
• *How did you decide what to do with each roll? Was this easy or difficult?*
• *What did you learn about yourself and your priorities during this game?*

the big boom!

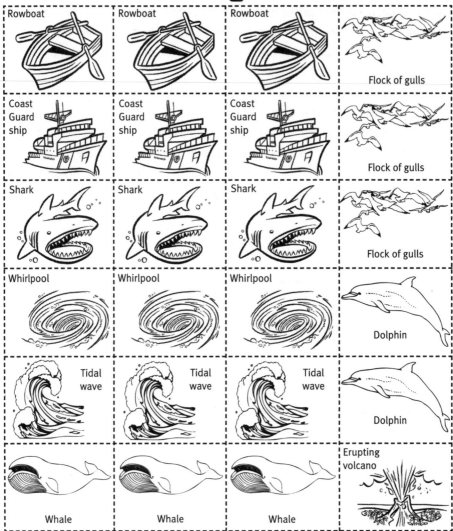

KEY

- **Rowboat**—move two spaces for every number on the die for the duration of the game.
- **Coast Guard ship**—move three spaces for every number on the die for the duration of the game.
- **Shark**—start over on the island of Wooloba.
- **Whirlpool**—move back three spaces toward Wooloba.
- **Dolphin**—the dolphin carries you forward two extra spaces.
- **Tidal wave**—move back two spaces toward Wooloba.
- **Whale**—just hang out in your space.
- **Flock of gulls**—look out for the "white rain"! Step back a space to get out of the way.
- **Erupting volcano**—Oops! The game is over!

over·the·top

games

for youth ministry

group
quest
games

A·Hunting We Will Go!

OVERVIEW: Players will work together as they hunt for people, items, and experiences.

TIME INVOLVED: approximately 1 hour and 30 minutes

GROUP SIZE: from 8 to 40 participants

SUPPLIES: photocopies of "Can You Find It?" (pp. 47-48), video cameras, videotapes, TV/VCR, a few dollars for each student, pens and pencils

PREPARATION: Photocopy the "Can You Find It?" handouts (pp. 47-48). You'll need one copy for each group of four. Recruit several adult drivers to accompany scavenging groups.

The Game

Have students form groups of four, and explain that groups will be going on a crazy scavenger hunt. Give each group a "Can You Find It?" handout, and direct students' attention to the "Rules" section. Tell groups that they'll have one hour to get as many points as possible by locating the items on their lists. Tell them the exact time they need to return, and remind them that points will be deducted for each minute they're late. Ask groups to take a few minutes to decide on a "plan of attack," and then send them on their way.

When groups return, have them share what they found and any funny experiences they had along the way, then watch the videos together. Have groups tally their points, and then give all of the groups a huge round of applause for a great scavenging job!

For extra impact

Have groups discuss the following questions and then share their answers with the whole group. Ask:
- *How did you feel about this scavenger hunt?*
- *What was your craziest stop along the way?*
- *What strategies or plans did your group use in order to achieve success?*
- *How is this like making plans to succeed in real life?*

can you find it?

The object of this crazy scavenger hunt is to gain as many points as possible by locating the following items. Be sure to follow the rules to have a safe and fun hunting experience!

RULES

- You have exactly one hour to complete your hunt. For each minute your group is late, five points will be deducted from your final score.
- All driving must be done at a reasonable and safe speed, following all traffic laws.
- Driving will be done *only* by the designated adult driver.
- Your entire group must complete all challenges—you cannot split up at any time.
- If you are retrieving an item, you must have permission to take or buy the item.
- It is your group's responsibility to return all items to their owners at the end of the game.
- If you are retrieving a person, a photograph or videotape is not acceptable. You must have the actual person with you.
- All activities in the "Challenges" section must be documented on videotape.

ITEMS

- ❏ 1 Halloween napkin (10 points)
- ❏ 1 raw green bean (15 points)
- ❏ 1 Braille menu (20 points)
- ❏ 1 pig—no live ones, please! (20 points)
- ❏ 10 green marbles (20 points)
- ❏ 1 properly labeled container of coriander (20 points)

- ❏ 1 blue gumball from a gumball machine (25 points)
- ❏ 1 bowl of prepared green gelatin (30 points)
- ❏ 1 Batman yo-yo (35 points)
- ❏ 1 yellow submarine (40 points)
- ❏ 1 foam cup filled with lint or couch fuzz from someone's house (50 points)

PEOPLE

- A person who was not with the group at the beginning of the hunt. This person should be someone the group knows and trusts. If this person is under 18, he or she will need to get parental permission. (100 points)

  (Note: For every challenge this person participates in with the group, add five points to the group's total score.)

CHALLENGES

- Have someone give your group a guided tour of his or her back yard. (10 points)
- Slice a lemon, and have each person sink his or her teeth into a slice and hold it there for at least three seconds. (15 points per person)
- Do a back-rub or back-scratch circle for at least thirty seconds. (20 points)
- Have one group member pet a baby lamb or goat. (25 points)
- Work together to create your own greeting card for someone, and hand-deliver it. (25 points)
- Have someone give your group a guided tour of his or her freezer. (30 points)
- Have a prayer time at any point during your travels. (30 points)
- Have a group conversation with either a four-legged animal or a statue. (30 points)
- In a park or a playground, have the entire team play two rounds of Duck, Duck, Goose. (35 points)
- Have all the members of your group try one food from a restaurant or deli that no one in the group has ever tasted. (40 points)
- At a fast-food restaurant or a convenience store, do the Macarena or the hokeypokey with at least one employee joining you. (50 points)
- With parental permission, interview a child between the ages of two and six about a current news issue. The interview must last at least twenty seconds. (50 points)
- Along with one other person who will not be returning with your group, blow bubbles. Each person must have a bubble in the air at the same time. (60 points)
- At someone's house, take turns riding on a wheeled object, such as a tricycle or a wagon. Make at least two laps around the house. Be careful not to damage any property or toys. (60 points)
- In a public establishment with the management's permission, have the entire group sing a song over the public-address system. The song should last at least ten seconds. (60 points)

Alïen Inuasïon

OVERVIEW: Students will work in teams to identify an alien spy within their midst and simultaneously work to crack an alien code and decipher the alien message.

TIME INVOLVED: 30 minutes to 1 hour

GROUP SIZE: from 10 to 100 or more participants

SUPPLIES: playing cards (with 1 joker), large sheet of newsprint, tape, marker, pads of paper, pencils, chair

PREPARATION: Gather together playing cards so that there will be one card per student and so that there is one joker in the deck. If you have more than fifty-three students, add cards (not jokers) from other decks of playing cards.

Write the following "alien message" on the piece of newsprint and tape it up on the wall: NBY MOHFCABN IH YULNB CM NII VLCABN!

Set out pens, pencils, and pads of paper. Put the chair in a corner of the room facing the wall.

The Game

When students arrive, tell them that the government has recently gotten word of a planned alien invasion of planet Earth. And even worse, the government is suspicious that an alien spy has already infiltrated society!

Explain that the secret alien spy has no distinct physical shape or look. Rather, he or she has the nasty habit of "borrowing" other people's bodies on the planet the aliens are attempting to dominate. The secret alien *does* have one distinctive trait that makes him or her recognizable. The bright light of the earth's sun makes the alien blink his or her eyes constantly. On the secret alien's home planet, blinking is considered an impolite gesture and is avoided in public, so the alien spy is rather shy about his or her blinking habit.

Divide all of the students into alien-hunting teams of five. (If you have a smaller group, teams can be as small as two students each.) Let students know that they'll have two jobs. The first is to identify the alien spy (one of the students), and the second is to crack the alien code in order to decipher the alien message uncovered by the government. The alien message *must* be correctly decoded before the alien spy can be captured. Alien teams can split up into different roles, some members focusing on decoding the alien message while the others work on tracking down the alien by mingling with the other alien hunters. Or, if they'd like, they can alternate roles as code crackers or alien trackers.

Explain that the secret alien spy must blink at least once every ten seconds making him or her easy to identify—but there's a catch. The alien spy can freely move around the group exchanging bodies at will. If the secret alien fears capture, he or she only needs to secretly and lightly tap another person three consecutive times. As soon as this happens, an immediate transition of personality should take place. The person tapped now becomes the secret alien and must begin blinking every ten seconds. The new alien is not allowed to "tag-back" the former alien—as soon as he or she passes on the alien identity, the former alien must immediately go through the process of "re-humanization."

To be re-humanized, the former alien needs to go to the chair in the corner facing the wall and sit there (without looking around) for one full minute. Afterward, the former alien may re-enter the game as a regular alien hunter.

Once an alien-hunting team correctly decodes the alien message, all of the students can work together to identify and capture the alien spy by tapping him or her on the shoulder and calling out "Caught ya!" Warn students, though, that if a student guesses incorrectly and accidentally captures an alien hunter, he or she cannot guess again—but must simply try to help out the other alien hunters.

Ask students if they have any questions about the rules you've explained so far. Once you're done answering questions, shuffle the deck of cards and pass out one card to each student. Instruct them to look at their cards without revealing them to others. The student with the joker is the alien spy. After students have looked at the cards, collect them and invite students to get started on the game.

As the game leader, station yourself near the alien message and pass out pens or pencils and pads of paper to students who come over to start working on the code. As students work on the code, feel free to give them hints that will help them decipher the solution. (A good first hint would be to ask them if they've thought of writing out the alphabet.)

So that you're equipped to help students, here's an explanation of the code. The code can be cracked by writing out the alphabet along the edge of a piece of paper then writing it out again along the edge of a second sheet of paper. By laying one paper on top of the other, with the edge of the paper underneath still showing, the two alphabets will both be visible next to each other. The paper underneath will become the "solution" paper and it simply needs to be moved so that the "G" on the solution paper is aligned with the "A" on the paper laying on top of it, which will become the "code" paper. The remaining letters of the alphabet (U through Z) must be assigned to the code alphabet, corresponding with the beginning six letters of the alphabet on the solution paper (as shown below). The alphabet on the solution paper contains the letters to be used for the solution while the alphabet on the code paper represents the code used by the aliens in their message.

LEADER TIP

If students are unable to make any progress on the code, show them how to create the two alphabet lists on paper and encourage them to begin sliding the top sheet along the bottom sheet alphabet. Prompt them to try and find a match that would turn the coded message into an English solution.

THE CODE

SOLUTION ALPHABET   **CODE ALPHABET**

A B C D E F G H I J K L M N O P Q R S T U V W X Y Z

U V W X Y Z A B C D E F G H I J K L M N O P Q R S T U V W X Y Z

The alien code can be deciphered by replacing all code letters with the corresponding solution letters as indicated below.

CODED MESSAGE:
    N B Y   M O H F C A B N   I H   Y U L N B   C M   N I I   V L C A B N !
SOLUTION:
    T H E   S U N L I G H T   O N   E A R T H   I S   T O O   B R I G H T !

Once the alien message is correctly deciphered and the alien is captured, end the game by congratulating all of the students on their teamwork.

impact

For extra

Use this game to prompt students to think about low self-esteem. Ask:
- *The alien in this game had a blinking problem—a problem the alien was embarrassed by. Can you relate to this?*
- *How does it feel to have something about yourself that you are afraid others won't like?*
- *What types of worries about traits or situations can cause someone to have low self-esteem?*
- *How can we encourage people who have low self-esteem?*

Art Auction

OVERVIEW: Participants will work together to guess the connection between ten bidders at an auction and the objects they bid on.

TIME INVOLVED: 30 minutes to 1 hour

GROUP SIZE: from 15 to 50 participants

SUPPLIES: gardening gloves, small flower pot, flower, large hat, bag of flour, ice-cream cone or piece of cake, poster or picture depicting the desert; batch of bread dough, stuffed animal deer or a picture of a deer (doe, not buck or stag), marching band uniform, drum and drumstick, can of beets, 2x4 board (wood), plate, a few pieces of Swiss cheese, "For Sale" sign, toy sailboat, wrapping paper, box, bow, tape, CD player, rap CD, carrots, knife, cutting board, diamond ring (or a fake imitation), brushes and combs or rollers, plush bunny rabbit, long table, ten numbered index cards, podium, ten chairs

PREPARATION: Set up a stage area with ten chairs in a row, the podium in the center, and the long table on the other side of the podium. Set the ten art objects described on the Bidder and Object Key (p. 54) in any order, and place a numbered index card in front of each object. Set up audience chairs for the students facing the stage area.

Before the game, select ten volunteers and assign a bidder identity to each of them. Make sure they are each costumed appropriately and with any needed personal props as indicated on the Bidder and Object Key. Tell each bidder what his or her art object is, and instruct students to keep this a secret. Instruct bidders that during the game they are to answer questions about their assigned character—they can create a personality for themselves—but must not deviate from the basic identity and actions assigned to them. It is also important that they not directly refer to any of the objects up for bid or use words (such as "flower") that would give away their object (such as the bag of "flour").

The Game

When participants arrive, welcome them formally to the auction in your best British accent. Introduce yourself as the auctioneer, invite the audience to be seated, and call the ten bidders to take seats (randomly) in the ten seats on the stage area.

Explain to the audience that an illustrious auction has just ended and it is their job to try to match up the objects with the bidders who bought them. They must work together to come up with questions for the bidders in an effort to get information that will help them guess which item each bidder bought in the auction. Audience members cannot ask any questions that directly deal with any of the objects up for bid—they must stick to questions about the bidders.

First take a moment to explain what each numbered art object is and then invite audience members to discuss ideas and begin their questioning. Every question must initially be addressed to you, the auctioneer, and if it is deemed an appropriate question, you then ask the question of the intended bidder.

This questioning process will continue until the audience members feel they've reached a consensus on which bidders bought which objects. A representative from the audience must then address the auctioneer and guess the buyers of *all ten* objects. If any of their guesses are wrong, simply tell them that they are incorrect and must guess again—but do *not* tell them which of their guesses were incorrect. They must simply try to guess again by asking bidders more questions and reconfiguring their pairing of all ten objects and bidders until they are all correct.

> **LEADER TIP**
>
> To create a glamorous auction atmosphere, use candlesticks, serving trays with finger foods and sparkling grape juice, and play classical music.

Once the audience has correctly guessed all ten pairs, congratulate them on a job well done.

impact

Use this game to begin a discussion about stereotypes and first impressions. Ask:

- *Can you tell a lot from just looking at a person?*
- *Have you ever been mistaken by a first impression?*
- *What's a good way to meet new people, especially if they're not the types of people you usually meet?*

BIDDER AND OBJECT KEY

BIDDER	ART OBJECT
Gardener with a large hat and gardening gloves, endlessly potting a *flower*	Large, well-marked bag of *flour*
Person who loves *dessert* and is eating an ice-cream cone or piece of cake	Poster or picture featuring the southwestern *desert*
Baker kneading fresh bread *dough*	Stuffed animal deer or a picture of a deer (*doe*)
Marching band drummer who from time to time *beats* his or her drum	Can of *beets*
Person who is restless and *bored* and keeps saying things like "There's nothing to do."	2x4 lumber *board*
Religious person acting very *holy*	Plate full of *holey* Swiss cheese
Realtor with a "For *Sale*" sign	Toy boat with a *sail*
Parent *wrapping* a large box with paper and a bow for his or her child	CD player playing *rap* music.
Cook cutting up *carrots* for soup	Very large twenty-*karat* ring
Beautician who loves doing other people's *hair*	Stuffed animal rabbit (*hare*)

Fact or Fiction?

OVERVIEW: Students will work in small groups to decipher truths and lies in other groups' presentations.

TIME INVOLVED: 30 minutes to 1 hour (depending on group size)

GROUP SIZE: from 8 to 60 or more participants

SUPPLIES: index cards, envelopes, pens or pencils, paper

PREPARATION: Before the game, write out True/False Codes on the index cards, one for each group of six students. A True/False Code should be any combination of twelve T's and F's. These should be written carefully so that they cannot be seen through the back of the index cards. Here are a few examples of True/False Codes:

T T T F T F F F T T T F T

F T F F F F T F T T T T

T F T F T F T T T F F T

Put each of the True/False Code index cards in an envelope.

The Game

Divide students into groups of six, and assign each group a number. (If you have fewer than twenty-four students, divide them into groups of four or five.) Explain that each group will have the challenge of presenting an impromptu conversation to the other groups. Each conversation will include true statements and false statements, based on the True/False Code each team will receive. The T's and F's on the code determine the order of true or false statements they must make in their conversation. Each group will select its own topic for their conversation, such as likes and dislikes, movies and TV shows, sports, or childhood memories.

Pass out the True/False Code envelopes as well as paper and pens or pencils to the groups, and invite them to spread out around the room so that they can look at their secret code and discuss what they'll say in their conversations. Explain that the groups need to present their conversations standing in a line, with

LEADER TIP

Some groups may need help selecting a topic or planning the conversation. Make yourself available to help the various groups in their brainstorming efforts.

the first person saying the first true or false statement indicated by their code, the second person saying the second true or false statement indicated by their code, and so on. Once they go through their line, they'll start over again at the front of the line for the final six statements.

Give students a few minutes to discuss and practice their Fact or Fiction conversations. When they're ready, explain that there will be several rounds of the game. For each round, groups will pair up and take turns presenting their conversations to each other, based on their secret codes. Each group can take notes during the other group's conversation. After they've presented their conversations, they'll spend a few minutes in their own groups trying to decide which statements from the other team's conversations were true or false statements, and attempting to write down what they think the other group's True/False Code is.

After all of the groups have seen the presentations of all of the other groups, they'll have a chance to guess what the other teams' True/False Codes were.

Ask the students if they have any questions. Once you've answered any questions, begin the game by telling each group who they should pair up with. (For example, group one and two should go together, group three and four should go together, and so on.) Once groups are paired up, start the first round. Continue to begin and end rounds until all of the groups have been paired together.

When the rounds have ended, give the students ten minutes to discuss in their groups what their final guesses will be for all of the other groups' twelve-letter True/False Codes. Then invite all of the groups to take turns guessing each other's codes, then revealing what their own True/False Code was. Conclude the game by congratulating the students on their great teamwork!

impact

for extra

Wrap up this game with a discussion about lying. Ask:
- *How hard is it to know if someone is telling a lie or telling the truth?*
- *What are some reasons that people lie?*
- *Is there such a thing as a little "white" lie? Or are all lies the same?*
- *Is it ever OK to lie? Explain.*
- *What are the negative consequences of lying?*
- *What are some benefits of telling the truth?*

Hulk Hunt

OVERVIEW: Players will search in teams for a volunteer painted completely green and attempt to capture his image in photographs, sound bites, or video footage without being tagged by the "Hulk"!

TIME INVOLVED: 30 minutes to 1 hour

GROUP SIZE: from 20 to 60 participants or more

SUPPLIES: whistle, green washable face paint and tattered clothing, several pairs of binoculars, instant-print cameras, portable tape recorders, video cameras, instant-print film, blank audio and video cassettes

PREPARATION: This outdoor activity requires a large wooded playing area, such as a campground, retreat center, or park. You will also need the assistance of an adult volunteer who doesn't mind getting grungy and green. Beforehand, disguise your Hulk with green face paint. Use the recipe provided at right or mix washable, nontoxic finger paint or poster paint with a small amount of glycerin or cold cream, and paint the volunteer's face, neck, and arms. Hair could be turned green using the powdered-drink-mix dying method. The hulk should dress in tattered clothing and be prepared to hide out among the trees and brush. Have instant-print cameras, video cameras, tape recorders, and tapes ready for distribution when participants arrive.

> **LEADER TIP**
>
> To make your own face paint, mix 1 teaspoon cornstarch with ½ teaspoon of water and ½ to 1 teaspoon of cold cream. Add a few drops of green food coloring. If the mixture is too thick, thin it with a few drops of water.
>
> To remove the face paint, use a deep-cleansing face soap. If traces of green remain, use dish soap or a mixture of equal parts lemon juice, astringent, and baking soda. Apply with a cotton ball, avoiding the eye area, and then rinse.
>
> Hair can be temporarily dyed green by adding a package of regular (not sugar-free) lime powdered-drink mix to hair conditioner. Add a small amount of water. Comb the paste through hair. Wrap hair in plastic wrap for twenty to thirty minutes. Rinse. Color should wash out of hair in one to several washes.

The Game

When teenagers arrive, ask them to form small groups. There should be no more than six or seven in a group. Evenly distribute binoculars, loaded video and instant-print cameras, and tape recorders among the groups.

Explain that groups will be searching to find and document evidence for the existence of the green Hulk. Just as the "Incredible Hulk" made appearances when he became angry, students could try and force the green giant from hiding by provoking

> **LEADER TIP**
>
> This game could easily be adapted to a Search for Sasquatch. Check with local rental or costume shops and locate a gorilla costume. Substitute a yeti for the Hulk, sending participants on a search for the hairy beast!

him. You may need to remind some students that this is a game meant for fun, and the provocation should be tasteful and in good humor. Be sure students know the boundaries of the playing area. Players should try to locate the Hulk and get close enough to record or photograph his image. If a student is tagged by the Hulk, that person must forfeit whatever he or she is carrying—camera, pictures, binoculars, and so on.

Blow a whistle when it is time for teams to return to the meeting area, and then give groups time to share their findings.

impact

Since the Incredible Hulk appeared when he became upset, this lighthearted game could preface a discussion about the more delicate issue of dealing with anger in a positive way. Ask volunteers to read Ephesians 4:26-27; Proverbs 14:29; and James 1:19-20 aloud. Ask:

- *What things provoke you to anger?*
- *Can anger ever be a good thing? Explain.*
- *What do you think angers God?*
- *How can anger be dealt with in a way that God approves of?*
- *What is the best way to get over angry feelings toward someone who has hurt you?*
- *What are some phrases that heal wounded relationships?*

M.I.M.E. Detective Agency

OVERVIEW: Students will create and then solve a mystery by miming their guesses to the game leader.

TIME INVOLVED: 45 minutes to 1 hour

GROUP SIZE: from 6 to 50 participants

SUPPLIES: yellow, white, and green index cards; pens; adhesive name tags; paper grocery bag; large manila envelope with the word "solution" written on it; stool; table; 10 to 20 creative pieces of junk, odds and ends, or household appliances (such as a plunger, a tennis racket, ice skates, a box of gelatin, a toaster, a barbell, a butter knife, a chocolate bar, a muffin pan, a ball of yarn, cotton balls, lipstick, a soccer ball, a can of pop, or a pair of pantyhose)

PREPARATION: Before the game, notify students that they should come to the event with a silly criminal identity. Have them think of a crazy name and even some creative costuming in advance. For example, they could be "Angling Annie," a criminal dressed in fishing gear, or "Bubble Gum Bubba," a criminal dressed in hot pink and chomping on bubble gum.

Prepare the game area by setting the various objects and odds and ends around the perimeter of the room. Place the stool in the center of the meeting area and the table with nametags and pens near the entry of the room.

The Game

As students arrive, have them write their wacky criminal names on name tags and put them on. Begin the game by giving students fifteen minutes to mingle around the room in an effort to get to know everyone's criminal identity and also to observe all of the various objects placed around the room.

When time is up, tell the students that they are each to create a murder mystery scenario using the people and objects in the room. They should silently think of a murderer, a victim, and a silly murder weapon. (The weapon must be one of the objects in the room.) If they'd like, they can walk around the room a bit to refresh their memories on criminal names and the murder weapons in the room.

Pass out a white, a yellow, and a green index card to each student, and ask them to write the three elements of their mystery scenario on the cards. On the white card, they should write the name of the murderer; on the yellow card, they should write the name of the victim; on the green card, they should name the object used as the murder weapon.

When students are done writing, collect all of the cards, place them in the grocery bag, shake it up, and then draw one card of each color from the bag, being careful not to reveal their contents to any of the students. These three cards will now serve as the solution to the mysterious whodunnit. Review the cards, and then place them in the manila "solution" envelope. Keep the envelope with you at all times.

Take a seat on the stool, and invite the students to gather around. Introduce yourself as the Detective General of the M.I.M.E. (Mostly Incompetent Mime Egotists) Detective Agency, and let them know that they are all Junior M.I.M.E. Detectives on their first case. Say: **As you know, the founder of our esteemed M.I.M.E. Detective Agency, Ronny Mime, decided that mimes would make the best undercover detectives because they didn't spend time in useless chatter. Because of this, Mr. Mime developed the process of Mime-o-forensics: solving a crime in complete silence.**

Tell all of the students that as Junior M.I.M.E. Detectives, their job is to try to guess the solution to a mysterious murder case using the identities of the people in the room as the murderer and victim and the objects along the perimeter of the room as the murder weapon. To solve the mystery, Junior Detectives must simply ask you basic yes or no questions.

The challenge of the game, though, is that all questioning must be done completely in mime. This questioning can't be done by pointing at people or objects—it must be done by describing the names of criminals or the objects through actions and demonstrations, gestures, and facial expressions.

As the Detective General, your job will simply be to nod "yes" or "no" to the students in answer to their mimed questions. If you don't understand what they're communicating, simply furrow your brow and shrug your shoulders to communicate your consternation. During the game, make sure that you keep track of which students correctly guess the various parts of the solution.

Explain to all of the Junior Detectives that once a student correctly guesses all three elements of the mystery solution, he or she becomes a game mole. You will indicate to a student that he or she guessed all elements correctly by covertly tapping each of your shoulders. At that point, the game mole should now simply try to confuse the game as much as possible by asking the Detective General questions that will throw the others off the trail.

Once there are six game moles, the game is over! (If the group is small, then only two or three moles are needed to end the game.)

When you're done explaining the rules, ask the students if they have any questions about the game. When there aren't any more questions, instruct the students to start miming, and begin the game!

When the game ends after six students solve the mystery, congratulate all of the Junior Detectives on a job well done, and reveal the solution to the mystery.

LEADER TIP

If you have more than fifteen students, you may want to select one or two Assistant Detective Generals who will be able to assist you in the questioning and answering process. Your team of Detective Generals *is* allowed to whisper back and forth to each other in order to keep track of which junior detectives are guessing correctly.

LEADER TIP

You may want to keep track of the names of the game moles by writing them down on a piece of paper.

impact

Use this game to segue into a discussion on the power of words. Ask:

- *Have you been in a situation where words just didn't work?*
- *Describe times when words are not necessary (like when you're comforting someone who has suffered a loss). When else?*
- *Do words have power? Explain.*
- *Why should we choose our words wisely?*

Missing Person

OVERVIEW: Players will investigate the case of a missing person.

TIME INVOLVED: 30 to 45 minutes

GROUP SIZE: from 5 to 40 participants

SUPPLIES: paper, pencils, markers, newsprint, tape, envelope, photocopy of "The Case of the Missing Meter Maid" (pp. 62-63)

PREPARATION: Photocopy "The Case of the Missing Meter Maid" (pp. 62-63), and cut apart the sections. Place the Mystery Solution in a sealed envelope.

The Game

Have students form five small groups (a group can be as small as one student).

Say: **Today we have a mystery to solve. It's the Case of the Missing Meter Maid. Myrna, the aforementioned meter maid, was reported missing earlier today by her sister, Mary. Mary, who molds marbles down at the old Marbleworks Factory, said Myrna missed her lunch date with Mary, which is something that never happens. Obviously, there's more to this mystery than meets the eye!**

Give each group a section of "The Case of the Missing Meter Maid" handout (pp. 62-63). Also give each group a supply of paper and pencils, a large sheet of newsprint, and a marker.

Explain that each group now has an identity and a set of clues and facts that pertain to the mystery. Each group's set of clues contains different information. To

(continued on p. 64)

the case of the missing meter maïd

Police Detectives

- Myrna was reported missing at approximately 6:15 p.m., Thursday, August 24, after her sister Mary became worried when Myrna missed a luncheon engagement and did not call to explain why.
- On the morning of Thursday, August 24, merchants reported seeing a stranger in a blue convertible parked on Main Street. Myrna was seen talking to this unidentified man, but no citation was recorded in her log book.
- The officer sent to interview Myrna's neighbors was unable to complete his assignment. He severely injured his big toe when he stubbed it on a "For Sale" sign in Myrna's neighbor's yard, and was rushed to the hospital.

Myrna's Co-Workers in the Meter Maid Division

- Sally Citation reports that Myrna decided on the morning of Thursday, August 24, to take the afternoon off, since she had approximately seven years of vacation time saved up. Sally quoted Myrna as saying, "I just need to cool off."
- Thomas Ticket, Myrna's supervisor, said he granted Myrna's request for the afternoon off because the meter maids don't usually write many tickets in the afternoons anyway. After all, when it's so hot, people generally stay at home.
- Some of Myrna's co-workers were not available for comment due to an unexpected ticket-writing emergency. It seems an unusually large number of cars were illegally parked near the Bijou Theater as the public rushed to view the *Star Wars* movie festival.

Mary, Myrna's Sister

- Mary says that Myrna hasn't missed one of their lunch dates in years, because Myrna knows it's the only chance she has of finding out about all the new marble colors being mixed at the Marbleworks.
- Mary also says that Myrna hasn't been acting like herself lately. She seems distracted— like she's not really interested in what Mary has to say. Mary says that's just not like her. She wondered if Myrna was angry with her.
- Mary said that she's been calling her sister at least seven times a day for the past three years (when Mary began her exciting career at the Marbleworks). Only recently has Myrna been acting annoyed, even to the point of saying last week, "Enough already with the marbles!"

Myrna's Neighbors

- Bertha Biddy, who lives across the street from Myrna, saw a blue convertible drive slowly by Myrna's house in the early afternoon of Thursday, August 24. She reports locking all of her doors and windows for fear that the driver was "casing the neighborhood."
- Sgt. John J. Strictly, retired, who lives next door to Myrna, reports that he saw her leave her house at approximately 3 p.m., August 24, carrying a large plastic bag which appeared to be heavy.
- Bertha Biddy, as she peeked out from behind her curtains, saw that Myrna's garage door was open, and that Myrna appeared to be sorting clothes into piles.

Town Merchants

- Patsy Pansy, owner of the floral shop, said she saw Myrna stop and smell the roses as she passed by at approximately 3:15 p.m., Thursday, August 24. She was carrying a heavy-looking plastic bag. When asked why she wasn't in uniform, Myrna smiled and murmured something about meeting a man named Luke.
- Teddy Teller, head clerk at the bank, said he saw Myrna come into the bank just before closing on Thursday, August 24. He did not think she was carrying a plastic bag. According to the teller who waited on her (who could not be reached for comment because he was fired for insubordination), Myrna withdrew twenty dollars and asked what time the bank opened in the morning.
- Cathy Sweets, owner of the candy store next to the movies, said that Myrna stopped in briefly on Thursday, August 24. She bought a bag of caramel popcorn.

Mystery Solution

Myrna wasn't missing at all. She took the afternoon off because it was 102 degrees outside and her navy blue uniform made it seem even hotter. So she went home, changed, and walked downtown. The bag she was carrying contained old clothes to be dropped off for the church garage sale. The man in the blue convertible was just asking directions since he will be moving to town with his family next month. Myrna told him about the house next door to hers that's for sale. As for needing to cool off, Myrna decided to go to the *Star Wars* marathon at the movies, since the theater is air-conditioned.

When asked why Myrna skipped her lunch date with Mary, Myrna replied, "We have lunch on Fridays, not Thursdays! Honestly, I think that sister of mine is losing her marbles!"

solve the mystery, each group will have a chance to interview every other group. The catch is that each group can ask another group only three questions. Therefore, each group must work together carefully before the interviews to come up with pertinent questions to ask.

Clarify that after each interview, groups will add the new information they've obtained to their set of clues. Groups can keep track of their clues both on the paper provided or by hanging a sheet of newsprint to the wall to make a timeline about Myrna's activities.

After each group has interviewed every other group, they will come up with a hypothesis about what happened to Myrna. Then groups will share their ideas and information and decide on a solution to the mystery.

Give groups time to read their set of clues and prepare questions for their first interview. Then let groups pair up and identify who their groups represent. Each group will ask its three questions, and the other group will answer only those questions, without divulging their clues unless they actually answer a question. Then groups will separate to add this new information to their sets of clues. After groups have decided which questions to ask during the next interview, have each group pair up with a new group for the second interview.

Continue the process until each group has interviewed every other group. Then give students time to complete their final hypotheses. Let each group present its solution to the mystery, explaining their supporting evidence. Other groups should take notes so they can discuss the case after all groups have presented.

LEADER TIP

For extra fun, have a volunteer come into the room to play Myrna. She can read the solution herself and answer students' questions. It's OK that she won't know all of the answers to students' questions, since some of the information groups were given was superfluous, just as in a real investigation.

Once all the solution hypotheses are presented, let the participants debate any discrepancies they noted. Groups will likely disagree with each other and come up with different solutions, since they probably will not have shared all of their clues during the interviews.

Groups can now share all of their clues and information with each other. Then groups must come up with one solution to the mystery that a majority of game participants support. When players have voted on one solution, open the envelope with the answer to the riddle and read aloud the actual solution to the mystery.

impact

To spark discussion after this game, use the following questions. Ask:

- *What was it like to try to solve this mystery without having all of the information?*
- *How did your own preconceived ideas influence your judgment in solving this mystery?*
- *How do preconceived ideas affect you in real life?*

Pirate Plunder

OVERVIEW: Teenagers will work together to solve a mystery by examining a map of prints. They will determine what the prints represent and in what order they were made.

TIME INVOLVED: approximately 30 minutes

GROUP SIZE: 8 to 50 or more participants

SUPPLIES: large sheet of butcher paper (10 to 15 feet long); several colors of finger paint; paper; pens or pencils; the following track objects: horseshoe, soccer ball, large tire, dog (or potato cut into a stamp of a dog footprint), football, hose, roller skates (or inline skates), bicycle

PREPARATION: At least one day prior to the game, set aside a few hours to create a Pirate Track Map on the piece of butcher paper. Use the finger paints and the track objects to create layers of tracks on the map in the order indicated by the chart on page 66. Create a crazy quilt of tracks, progressing the length of the paper from the left side of the paper to the right. These tracks must be made on the paper one set at a time. Let each set of tracks dry thoroughly before moving to the next set. Also, make sure to wash each object after you make the tracks with it.

Tracks should vary in their patterns—some can proceed in a straight line, others can meander back and forth across the paper. It is important that each layer of tracks at some point overlaps atop the layer made prior to it. However, be careful that they don't overlap *so* much that they are no longer identifiable.

As you create your Pirate Track Map and as students play the game, keep the chart below handy as your "solution" to the mystery. This chart lets you know in which order you should lay tracks, and will serve as your reference when players make guesses about the order of the tracks. Once the Pirate Track Map is done and has dried, hang it up on the wall in your meeting area.

ORDER STOLEN	TRACKING OBJECT	REPRESENTING
1	Horseshoe	Horse
2	Soccer ball	Soccer ball
3	Large tire	Tire or car
4	Dog (or potato stamp of dog footprints)	Dog
5	Football	Football
6	Hose	Snake
7	Roller skates or inline skates	Pair of skates
8	Bicycle	Bicycle

The Game

When students arrive, tell them that a crew of evil pirates pillaged the town as they slept last night, stealing valuables and even pets! However, the pirates were very messy and left tracks of all the objects as they took them back to their ship.

Explain to the students that their job is to examine the Pirate Track Map on the wall and use it to determine the order of the tracks and then to identify which object or animal made each track. They'll be able to determine the order of the tracks by examining the places that tracks overlap and identifying which tracks were probably made first, second, third, and so on. Give students paper and pencils to record their findings.

In order to solve the Pirate Plunder mystery, students must work together as a large group to come up with a solution they all unanimously agree on before presenting it to you. If they guess any part of the order incorrectly, don't reveal which part of their guess was incorrect—just tell them they need to try again. If they identified one or more of the objects incorrectly, give them some hints to help them out,

> **LEADER TIP**
>
> If your group is larger than twenty participants, you may want to divide them into several smaller groups of ten to twenty who will work together to come up with solutions to the puzzle. Each smaller group must reach its solution guesses unanimously.

and then have them guess again. Once the group correctly guesses the solution to the mystery, congratulate them for their excellent teamwork.

impact

for extra

Use this game to help your students explore what it means to follow in Jesus' footsteps. Ask:

- *What does it mean to follow in Christ's footsteps?*
- *Where did he walk—what things did he do and what kinds of people did he hang out with—that might be challenging for you to imitate?*
- *What are some examples of ways you follow in Christ's footsteps and minister to people and in places that may not be easy?*

Scavenging Engineers

OVERVIEW: Teams will create scavenger hunts for each other, then use the items they collect to build new creations.

TIME INVOLVED: approximately 1 hour

GROUP SIZE: from 10 to 40 participants

SUPPLIES: paper, pencils, items such as tape, string, rubber bands, or other common items found in the church

PREPARATION: none

The Game

Have players form two teams. If you have more than twenty participants, you may have students form more than two teams. Ideally, a team should have no more than ten students. Give each team a supply of paper and pencils.

Say: **Today we're going to create a team challenge. Your team will have ten minutes to take a quick survey of the church looking for small, medium, and even large items that can be collected by the other team. After your survey, you'll come back here and work together to create a list of objects the other team has to collect, just like in a scavenger hunt. Your list must include at least ten, but no more than twelve, objects of a variety of sizes. All of the objects must be things that can be easily found in this building or on the grounds.**

Next, explain this twist. After teams create their lists, they must decide what the other team can build from those objects. On a separate sheet of paper, each team needs to describe what they think the other team will or can build from the objects on their list. They should then draw a picture of what they think the other team will build. Teams should keep their drawings a secret and should not reveal any information about what they drew. If needed, teams may go back and amend their lists to meet the needs of the object to be built.

Say: **At the end of the game, we'll compare the picture of what you thought the other team would build with the object they actually built. Let's get started on those lists!**

Give teams ten minutes to survey the church, looking for objects. Then have teams come back and create their lists. Objects students write on their list might include items such as crayons, markers, books, trash cans, brooms, mops, folding chairs, paper, cans of food, tape, yardsticks, fans, hymnals, and pots and pans.

When teams have finished writing, have them exchange lists with each other. Have each team read its list aloud. Make note of inappropriate or unobtainable objects, and also note any troublesome duplications. For example, if both teams have "crayons" on their lists, that's OK, since there are probably enough crayons in the building to go around. But both teams shouldn't list a "vacuum cleaner" if your church has only one. You be the judge.

The goal is for teams to actually be able to collect all of the objects on their lists, since they'll need them for the building stage of the game. If necessary, send teams back to the drawing board to revise their lists.

Give players a specified amount of time to collect their objects. Explain that teams must be back in your meeting area at the end of the specified time, whether or not they have collected all of the items on their lists. Let students figure out the best strategy for collecting the items—the less help you give, the more team members will learn to work together.

When groups return with their objects, let each team report on its success (or lack thereof) in finding the objects on its list. Then let the building begin! Team members should figure out on their own what they can build from their objects and then work together to assemble their new creation. Explain that all items collected must be used in the building project.

> **LEADER TIP**
>
> Encourage teams to record where they found each object collected, so they can return them to their proper places after the game. Also, caution students not to disturb any other church activities in progress as they search for the objects on their lists.

When students have finished building, let each team present its creation and explain what it is and how it could be used. Then let teams compare what they built with the picture the other team drew and see if their creation even comes close to what the other team thought they'd create.

For extra impact

Wrap up your time with a discussion about expectations. Ask:
- *How did the object you built compare to the other team's drawing?*
- *Was it easy or difficult to anticipate what the other team expected you to build? Explain.*
- *When do you have to consider others' expectations in real life?*
- *Is it a good or bad thing to try to live up to others' expectations? Why?*

Sting Operation

OVERVIEW: Players will try to guess the identity of an informant in their midst.

TIME INVOLVED: approximately 30 minutes

GROUP SIZE: from 12 to 40 participants

SUPPLIES: chairs, table, masking tape

PREPARATION: Set enough tables and chairs to seat one-fourth of the players. Arrange the tables and chairs to look like a restaurant. Nearby, have an area set up to serve as the kitchen. The kitchen can be as simple as an area marked off with masking tape.

The Game

Have students form four groups: the FBI, the Burgletons (an organized crime family), the politicians, and the owners and staff of a restaurant. All of the groups will interact at the restaurant.

Say: **Today we have a mystery to solve. Someone in one of your groups is an informant. That means that he or she is only pretending to be a loyal member of the group, but is meanwhile passing important information on to one or more of the other groups.**

Explain that you're going to read a script and each group is to silently act out the story as you read it. At the end of the story, each group will get one guess as to who the informant is. Clarify that even when participants are not acting in the story, they'll have to pay close attention to what's happening or they may miss a clue.

Direct each group to a section of the room. Explain that members of each group will move together and act out their group's parts together. For example, when the script says that the Burgletons arrive at the restaurant for dinner, all members of the Burgleton group will sit down at the restaurant table.

Read the following script in a voice loud enough for everyone to hear, pausing where indicated to give students time to play their parts.

"Inn the Know"

There was trouble in the big city. Someone was passing secret information, and no one knew who it was. Over in the FBI building, the agents were scratching their heads. (Pause.) *Every time they thought they were going to make an arrest in the Burgleton family, the Burgletons somehow knew what was coming.*

But the Burgletons were upset too. Back on their street corner, the Burgletons were shaking their fists (pause) *and wondering how the FBI knew what they were up to.*

Meanwhile, up in the mayor's mansion, the politicians were still smiling and shaking hands. (Pause.) *But behind the smiles, they were concerned because someone kept leaking stories to the news that the politicians were turning their heads and letting the Burgletons get away with their slimy crimes.*

Even the staff at the Inn the Know Restaurant could feel the tension. Sure, they still set the tables and swept the floors as usual (pause), *but they were worried because the FBI, the Burgletons, and the politicians all ate there. In fact, they just saw the FBI agents coming toward the restaurant for lunch.* (Pause.)

The restaurant staff hurried to seat the FBI agents, and handed them menus. (Pause.) "So what's good in the seafood department?" asked one agent, winking. (Pause.)

"Well, I hear the clams are really good today," replied a waiter.

"Are those clams in the shell or not in the shell?" asked the agent.

"I don't know," said the waiter. "I'll go check."

As the waiter went to the kitchen to check on the clams (pause), *the other waiters scurried around filling water glasses and bread baskets.* (Pause.) *The waiter came back and said the clams were not in the shell.* (Pause.) *The agent looked disappointed and said he'd have a hamburger instead. The waiters took everyone's order and went to get the food.* (Pause.)

As they waited, the agents shook their heads. (Pause.) "I just can't figure out how the Burgletons know our every move. They'd better not find out that we know about the fake money scheme." *The agents finished their meals and went back to the FBI building.* (Pause.)

A little while later, the Burgletons came into the restaurant for dinner. (Pause.) *The waiters really scurried around this time, 'cause it doesn't pay to make the Burgletons wait!* (Pause.) "Yo," said one Burgleton, winking. (Pause.) "What kinda seafood ya got today?"

"Oysters, I think," said a waiter.

"Are those oysters in the shell or not in the shell?"

"I don't know," said the waiter. "I'll go check."

So the waiter hurried back to the kitchen (pause) *as the Burgletons drummed their fingers on the table. Soon the waiter came back.* (Pause.) "The oysters are in the shell," said the waiter.

"Good, I like 'em in the shell." So the Burgleton brother ordered the oysters, and the waiters took all the orders (pause) and hurried back to the kitchen. (Pause.) When the food arrived, one of the brothers bit into his oyster. "Ugh!" he exclaimed, as he slammed down his fist. "This tastes rotten! I'm going to give that chef a piece of my mind!" He stood up and stormed to the kitchen while the rest of the Burgletons ate their food and discussed their business dealings.

At the end of the meal, Bobby said, "Yo, I think we oughta lay off that fake money scheme." All the other Burgletons nodded their heads. (Pause.) "Let's just stick with bribing the politicians for now." All the other Burgletons agreed as they got up to leave. (Pause.)

That night, the politicians stopped by the restaurant for a late-night snack since they had worked through dinner. (Pause.) As soon as they were seated (pause), the mayor asked, "What kind of seafood do you have tonight?" Then he winked. (Pause.)

"We have mussels," replied a waiter.

"Are those mussels in the shell or not in the shell?" asked the mayor.

"I don't know; I'll go check," said the waiter as he hurried to the kitchen. (Pause.) As they waited, the politicians smiled and shook the hands of everyone else in the restaurant. (Pause.)

The waiter came back (pause) and said, "The mussels are not in the shell."

"Never mind," sighed the mayor, "I'll have the soup." The waiters brought the soup (pause) and the politicians ate. (Pause.) As they ate, the mayor said, "We'd better find out who's leaking that information, and soon!" The other politicians nodded (pause) and then smiled. (Pause.) Then they went back to the mayor's mansion. (Pause.)

The waiters cleaned up the tables (pause) and swept the floors. (Pause.) Then they turned out the lights (pause) and locked up the restaurant. (Pause.)

The End.

After you finish reading the script, gather groups together in the restaurant area. Lead students in a round of applause for everyone's participation. Then have students discuss the following questions in their groups. After each question, invite groups to share their answers with the rest of the class. Let groups discuss each question until they agree on an answer. *Ask:*

- **Who, if anyone, received secret information in this story? Explain your answer.**
- **How was information passed from one group to another?**
- **Who was the informant?**

Once groups have reached a consensus on all three questions, reveal the answer.

Say: **The only group to receive secret information in this story was the Burgleton family. They learned that the FBI knew about their fake money scheme. But** there was actually an informant in each of the groups—they just all didn't receive information in this story. The person in each group who asked about the seafood was the informant in that group. The master informant was the restaurant cook. As waiters came in and out, the cook casually asked them what the people at the tables were talking about. That's how he got his information.

So when an informant asked about the seafood, and the unsuspecting waiter went back to ask the cook, the cook then knew an informant wanted information. If he had information to pass, the cook said the seafood was served in such a way as to conceal a message, such as in a shell. Then that's what the informant would order. Otherwise, the informants just ordered something else, and knew that no information would be passed. End of story.

For extra impact

Use this silly story to lead into a discussion about deceit. Ask:
* *Have you ever felt like you were being tricked or deceived? What was it like?*
* *How can you spot deceit?*
* *Is it ever OK for Christians to be deceitful? Defend your answer.*

Wall of Jericho

OVERVIEW: Participants will march around the church building seven times while navigating a variety of obstacles.

TIME INVOLVED: 30 to 45 minutes

GROUP SIZE: from 10 to 50 or more participants

SUPPLIES: sawhorses, coat racks, chair, tables, plastic hoops, a hose hooked up to a faucet (or water in a basin), water balloons or squirt guns, sidewalk chalk

PREPARATION: Set up this obstacle-course game outside of your church building. Set up the supplies listed above as obstacles along the perimeter of the church building right next to the wall. Have adult volunteers position themselves in windows with water balloons or squirt guns.

Label each obstacle with instructions for students (such as "crawl under," "crawl over," "step around," or "tiptoe"). Direct them to write their names on the wall with the sidewalk chalk. (Do this somewhere near the hose for easy cleaning.) Instructions must be followed by each student on every lap.

Ask one adult volunteer to remain at the starting line to keep track of the laps.

The Game

Explain to players that this is not a race against another team or a timed event. Instead, students must work together to simply make their way around the building seven times. The crucial element is that they each must have one hand on the wall of the building at all times (they can switch hands if needed). If a participant is caught taking his or her hand off the wall, that player must go back to the beginning and start the lap over.

For an added twist, select a few players who will have to make their laps in the opposite direction from the rest of the students. When players meet each other on their way around, they must figure out a way to pass each other without removing their hands from the wall.

LEADER TIP

Instruct youth leaders with water balloons to drop them so that they hit the ground *near* students instead of actually hitting students. This will avoid bruises—and will get the participants wetter!

Clarify that the game ends only when all players are back at the starting point after successfully completing seven laps. Start the players on their way at thirty-second intervals. They will probably bunch up rather quickly, but that can be part of the fun as well.

When all students are back from their seventh trip around, have them give a loud shout (like Joshua and his army in the Bible).

impact

For extra

Use this game to lead into a discussion of Joshua and the battle of Jericho. First have a student read aloud Joshua 6:3-5. Ask:

- *Why do you suppose God gave Joshua such detailed directions? Do you think the instructions are strange? Why or why not?*
- *If an angel came to you with some truly "out there" instructions, do you think you would follow them? Explain.*

over·the·top

games
for youth ministry

team challenge games

Autograph Hunter

OVERVIEW: Players will form teams and collect autographs from each other as they move through a shopping mall.

TIME INVOLVED: 45 minutes to 1 hour

GROUP SIZE: from 10 to 60 or more participants

SUPPLIES: pencils, paper, enough money to buy every teenager a drink in the food court

PREPARATION: Make arrangements for safe transportation to and from the shopping mall. Instruct teenagers to wear watches on the day of the event.

The Game

This game takes place in a shopping mall—the larger and busier the mall, the better. The point of the game is for each participant to collect as many autographs as possible from members of the opposing team. Think of it as a sort of scavenger hunt...but the goal is to get autographs, not pictures of the Backstreet Boys and green golf tees.

After transporting students to the mall's food court area—where a large congregation of teenagers won't draw undue attention—have players form two or more teams and synchronize their watches. Teams should be a maximum of twenty players each.

LEADER TIP: Respect stores and store personnel. Teenagers acting suspiciously in a retail store are a magnet for unwanted attention—especially from security personnel.

Say: **This game, "Autograph Hunter," is one of stealth, cunning, and team strategy. I'll go through the rules in a moment, but first let me explain the goal of the game: Each team will collect as many autographs as possible from members of the other team(s).**

Explain that at the end of the game, the spot where you're standing will be your meeting place. Everyone *must* come directly back so you can tally up scores and complete the second part of the game. Don't share what that "second part" is. Your goal is to get everyone rounded up again promptly; curiosity helps. Also, clarify that you, or another adult volunteer, will be in the meeting spot during the entire game in case any questions or emergencies arise.

Next begin explaining the rules of the game. First, clarify that players may *not* leave the mall for any reason. Should there be a fire, flood, or other incident in which mall authorities insist all patrons leave immediately, everyone *must* go immediately to a designated area just outside one of the mall entrances. (Be very clear about where this would be and emphasize the importance of following this rule.)

Make it clear that players must work together in pairs or trios with members of their teams. They are *not* allowed to travel alone during the game. Players will move from one store in the mall to another store at least once every five minutes, except for the Media King or Queen. Each team's King or Queen and his or her partner may stay in one place as long as desired. The role of the Media King/Queen is just to hide out. The other teams get *extra points* for finding them and getting their autographs.

Tell participants that there is to be no running—*ever*. The goal is stealth, not speed. And running or looking suspicious will only draw unwanted attention.

Explain that to get an autograph, participants must approach another player, get within six feet of the person, and ask, "May I have your autograph?" When asked for an autograph, players must comply by giving it (legibly). Participants (and those in their pair or trio) cannot ask for the autograph of someone who has just gotten theirs; they must wait at least five minutes before asking for that autograph in return.

Tell players that for each unique autograph collected from a member of an opposing team, their team gets two points. Each time an autograph is collected from an opposing team's Media King or Queen, ten points are awarded. The team with the most collected autographs at the end of the game receives an extra 20 points.

Explain that the game begins exactly five minutes after you dismiss teams from the food court. Also set an ending time at which everyone must return immediately to the food court. Tell players that scores will be tallied precisely ten minutes after the game ends. If team members haven't yet returned with their autograph sheet, their points will not be counted toward their team's total.

> **LEADER TIP**
>
> Remind players that they don't get points for repeated autographs—the goal is to get an autograph from each member of the other team.

Once you've explained all these rules, give teams five minutes to huddle, decide on their strategy, and select their Media King or Queen. Teams will want to keep the identities of their Media Kings or Queens secret. Distribute a piece of paper and pen or pencil to each teenager, and dismiss them to play the game.

When students return at the end of the game, have teams quickly total up their points. Have the team with the most points take soft drink orders from the other team's members and go buy the drinks. (Supply the money!)

Announce that this is the second part of the game: a reminder that in the kingdom of God the last shall be first! Once the winning team has served the others, invite them to order their own drinks. Then find seats in the food court where your group can share stories about what happened during the game.

impact

Use these questions to help prompt discussion. Ask:

- *How did it feel to be asked for an autograph in a public place? How do you think celebrities feel when they're asked for autographs? Why?*
- *If you could choose to be a world-famous celebrity or to live a quiet life, which would you choose? Why?*
- *Do you think fame and riches make people happy? Explain.*

Wrap up your discussion by inviting someone to read Ecclesiastes 2:1-11. Prompt some students to comment on how the Scripture affects their perspective of fame and wealth.

Conspiracy Theory

OVERVIEW: Students will work in teams to create fragments of a conspiracy about anti-gardening fanatics conspiring to take over the world. Teenagers will then work together to unravel the conspiracy fragments created by the other teams.

TIME INVOLVED: 45 minutes to 1 hour

GROUP SIZE: from 12 to 42 participants or more

SUPPLIES: newsprint, markers, paper, pencils, photocopies of "Conspiracy Rap Sheet" (p. 81)

PREPARATION: Make several photocopies of "Conspiracy Rap Sheet" (p. 81). Before students arrive, select a linkage list from which squads will create the conspiracy. A linkage list is a group of related words that are in a sequential order moving from beginning to end. On page 79, you'll find several examples of linkage lists—feel free to use one of these lists or create your own.

LINKAGE LIST #1	LINKAGE LIST #2	LINKAGE LIST #3	LINKAGE LIST #4
• Farmyard (first) • Henhouse (second) • Hens (third) • Laying hen (fourth) • Newly laid egg (fifth) • Baby chicks (sixth)	• Empty shopping cart (first) • Grocery store (second) • Vegetables (third) • Kitchen (fourth) • Skillet (fifth) • Frying vegetables (sixth) • Candlelit dinner for two (seventh)	• Luncheon menu (first) • Order ticket (second) • Glass of water (third) • Bowl of soup (fourth) • Steak and french fries (fifth) • Ice-cream sundae (sixth) • Paying a restaurant bill (seventh)	• Arriving at airport (first) • Checking in luggage (second) • Going through security checkpoint (third) • Going out to plane gate (fourth) • Handing ticket to attendant at gate (fifth) • Boarding the airplane and taking a seat (sixth) • Airplane taking off (seventh)

The Game

When participants arrive, have them form police squads—squads should be made up of two to six players. A minimum of six squads are needed for the game to work.

Welcome all of the new "detectives" to the police headquarters and let them know that a conspiracy is afoot! Say: **Two days ago, the FBI intercepted communication indicating that four internationally known anti-gardening fanatics, Honore Peu, Giovanni Three, Bonnie Bowzer, and Fritz Burger, have each arrived at JFK airport in New York City. These fanatics are known for some of the most brutal and violent acts ever to be inflicted upon helpless varieties of vegetables, flowers, and assorted fruit trees. In order to catch these four fanatics, we must determine what has happened between the time of the fanatics' initial entry into the country up until now.**

Pass out a "Conspiracy Rap Sheet" to each group, and give them a few minutes to read through the criminals' descriptions.

When students are done reviewing the rap sheet, secretly assign each squad one

> **LEADER TIP**
>
> To add ambience to the game, make the room look like a briefing room at a local police station. Add a box or two of donuts, a pot of coffee, and a police radio.

of the hints from the linkage list you selected or created. Make sure to write down which squad gets which word so that you're always aware of the correct order of linkage hints. When assigning the hints, make sure you mix up the order in which you assign them.

Give each squad of detectives a piece of paper, and instruct them to write a short fragment of what will become the complete conspiracy story line. Let them know that their story fragment must be centered around the linkage hint you assigned to their particular squad. Each conspiracy fragment must include at least two of the four garden fanatics and must explain a creative crime they participated in. Each fragment must also include a geographic location as well as a negative result of the crime committed by the fanatics. Conspiracy fragments should be colorful, memorable, funny, and short. For example, if a team's linkage hint was "swimming pool" they could write a conspiracy fragment like this:

Honore Peu and Bonnie Bowzer met up for a secret rendezvous at the local town swimming pool in Kankakee, Illinois. After relaxing a few hours in the sun, the pair disappeared. No one realized who they were until they were already gone—and by then it was too late. Peu and Bowzer had already dumped two hundred gelatin packets and thirty pounds of grapes into the pool's filter, causing several neighborhood swimmers to develop permanently dyed strawberry-kiwi-colored hair.

After squads finish writing their conspiracy fragments, they should keep them completely secret.

Once all of the squads have written their conspiracy fragments, the squads can begin to interrogate each other about the fragment of the conspiracy they know. However, students must work together in their squads to agree on their interrogation questions. Only one question at a time can be asked of another squad. After that question is asked, the questioning squad must move on to the next available squad, but may come back to that squad later. Squads must continue to rotate from one squad to the next as they work to learn and understand the various story fragments.

Each squad can use their own sheet of newsprint to keep track of the various things they learn from each squad. The students should try to find out who was involved in each conspiracy fragment, what they did, where they did it, and what the result was. They should also try to decipher what the linkage hint is that is hidden in the story. Squads should try to gain this information through a logical step-by-step pattern of questioning the other squads.

Once a squad thinks they've gotten the basic information needed about each

conspïracy rap sheet

NAME: **Honore Peu**

CRIME: Large tuber and vegetable mangler. Once Peu single-handedly chopped up twenty-three tons of prize-winning Irish potatoes that were being given to the Queen of England as a peace offering. All of the potatoes were mashed and cooked in a root beer and tomato sauce.

NAME: **Giovanni Giovanni Giovanni** *(a.k.a. "Giovanni Three")*

CRIME: Garlic thief. Last year, at the Cooking Grande Prix of Rome, Giovanni Three substituted horseradish for garlic. Two thousand Italian connoisseurs' palates were destroyed at this gathering. This was considered the worst mass murder of taste buds in the twenty-first century.

NAME: **Bonnie Bowzer** *(alias "Unhappy-Meal Bonnie")*

CRIME: Loves to ruin others' meals. Once she repackaged fifteen tons of Argentinean strawberries with an equal amount of rutabaga. These were sent to the health-conscious city of Kyle, Texas. Kyle regularly sponsors the official Texas Strawberry Festival. Last year it was attended by delegations of athletes from China, Norway, and Oklahoma. No one noticed the fruit switched with the vegetable until it was too late. Needless to say, international relationships *soured* after this event.

NAME: **Fritz Burger**

CRIME: Avocado hater. It seems that as a boy his mother believed in the wonderful healing properties of avocados. Regularly, after a morning run and a spinach-kale-avocado drink, he would be treated to an avocado and salt bath. Lunch consisted of an avocado and blueberry shake served with a side of mashed avocado on white crackers. Fritz would be sent to his regular afternoon nap with avocado slices placed on both eyelids to ensure a most restful experience. Fritz, as one might assume, began to dislike the avocado.

At Napa Valley's wine festival last year, Fritz secretly drained all the wine casks and replaced their contents with fermented avocado milk. Suffice it to say, the annual Napa Valley wine festival will not take place this year (or possibly ever again).

conspiracy fragment, they should attempt to put the fragments in the correct sequential order. To accomplish this, a team needs to be able to identify the linkage hint in each fragment and connect them in the correct logical order.

The solution of the conspiracy will be comprised of each correct conspiracy fragment placed in the sequential order of the linkage hints you gave to each team.

After squads have had at least thirty minutes to question the other squads and come up with their version of the conspiracy, have all of the students gather back together and invite the various squads to share their conspiracy theories with each other. When they've all shared, reveal the correct order (based on your linkage list hints), and applaud the students for their effort.

impact

For extra

Use this game to lead students in a discussion about gossip. Ask:
- *Have you ever witnessed gossip twisting facts into a full-blown story? How different was the story from the facts?*
- *How does gossip develop?*
- *Is there ever any good gossip or is it always bad?*
- *How is the conspiracy we created similar to the way gossip can get out of hand? How is it different?*

Indoor Olympics

OVERVIEW: Students will participate in a series of indoor "athletic" events.

TIME INVOLVED: 1 to 3 hours (depending on group size)

GROUP SIZE: from 8 to 32 participants or more

SUPPLIES: masking tape, empty plastic milk carton, 2-foot length of rope, colored crepe paper, 2 scarves, 1 winter hat, pair of goggles, 2 yardsticks, two 1x4-foot pieces of cardboard, chairs, telephone book, 2 pads of paper, pencils, 10 pieces of cardboard

PREPARATION: Before students arrive, set up the following athletic events. (A large meeting area, such as a gym or fellowship hall, works best for this game.)

Synchronized Hopscotch: Use masking tape to create four identical hopscotch grids on the floor. The grids need to be several feet apart. Set long lengths of colored crepe paper near each grid.

Ski Slalom: Use chairs to create a slalom-type course that students will weave in and out of. The course should be at least twenty feet in length. Set out a winter hat, a pair of goggles, two yardsticks to be used as poles, two scarves, and two 1x4-foot lengths of cardboard to be used as skis.

Telephone Book Relay: In another section, mark a starting line on the floor. About ten or fifteen feet away from the starting line, set two chairs. On one chair, place a telephone book. On the other chair, place a pad of paper and a pencil. Choose five businesses or people at random from the phone book, and write their names and phone numbers on a sheet of paper. You'll keep this paper as a master list. On another sheet of paper, simply list the names. Place the list of names on the chair with the phone book.

Milk Carton Relay: In another section, mark a starting and finish line about thirty feet apart from each other. Near the starting line, place an empty plastic milk jug with a 2-foot length of rope tied to the handle.

Judges' table: On the table, place ten pieces of cardboard on which you've written the numbers from one to ten. Also set out a pad of paper and pencils.

The Game

Gather students together. Say: **Welcome to our first annual Indoor Olympics! In this game, we'll all be from the same fictitious country.**

Let students brainstorm a country to be from. When they've decided, lead students through the course of events, explaining each area of competition. The individual events are as follows.

> **LEADER TIP**
>
> For timed events, feel free to adjust the time limits to fit the size of each event's "course."

• **Milk Carton Relay.** This will be a timed event. Team members will line up behind the starting line. The first contestant will tie the milk jug to one ankle, making sure the rope doesn't hang down and cause a tripping hazard. Then he or she will hop on that foot to the finish line and back, untie the milk carton, and pass it to the next person in line. If a team successfully completes the race in less than three minutes, the team will receive 100 points.

• **Telephone Book Relay.** This will be a timed event. Team members will line up behind the starting line. At your signal, the first person in line will run to the two chairs, kneel on the floor, and read the first name or business listed on the sheet. He or she will quickly look up the phone number of that person or business, and write it on the pad of paper.

If you are able to recruit a few volunteers to help with this game, give several of them the job of being timekeepers for the various events. This will make the judges' jobs a little easier.

LEADER TIP

Then the contestant will run back to the line and tag the next person, who will look up the second number and write it on the same sheet the first contestant wrote on, and so on. When the last contestant on the team has looked up and written a number, he or she will tear off the list of numbers and hand it to you, at which point you'll stop timing. You'll compare the list with your master list, and award points for correct numbers. If a team successfully completes the relay in less than three minutes, the team will receive 100 points. Ten points will be deducted for each mistake made.

• **Synchronized Hopscotch.** Each team member will hold a length of crepe paper and stand at the starting point of a hopscotch grid. At your signal, team members will simultaneously hop through the grid and back, artistically waving their lengths of crepe paper as they hop. Judges award points strictly on form, artistic impression, and crowd involvement. Judging will be based on a scale of 1 to 10, then multiplied by 10. For example, a judge may award an all-around score of 7, then multiply it for a total score of 70.

LEADER TIP

If you have an especially large group, simply create more teams of four. You could also create more events for students to rotate through. Extra events might include shooting basketballs through a hoop while blindfolded, bobsled races (where the bobsleds are cardboard boxes), and ice hockey (where the hockey sticks are brooms and mops and the puck is a roll of masking tape).

• **Ski Slalom.** This will be a timed event. Team members will line up behind the starting line. The first person in line will put on the winter hat and goggles. Then the contestant will use the scarves to tie the cardboard pieces to his or her feet, and will hold the yardsticks as poles. Team members will "ski" through the slalom course and back, then the next person will repeat the process. When the final team member has removed the skis, hat, and goggles, timing will end. If a team successfully completes the course in less than five minutes, the team will receive 100 points.

Have students form teams of four, and have teams number off. Have each team line up at an event. Each team will compete individually as the rest of the teams cheer them on. Teams will rotate events, with each team taking a turn at the judges' table.

One team will always be sitting at the judges' table to keep score. Judges will each score the Synchronized Hopscotch event individually and will total their score. For the other events, you will call out the times each team gets, and judges will keep track of teams' times. At the end of the game, team scores will be compiled, and total points for the country will be calculated.

Explain that if the country earns a gold-medal total of 1,500 points, they will receive a pizza party. If they earn a silver-medal total of 1,200 points, they will receive ice cream. And if they earn a bronze-medal total of 1,000 points, candy will be in order.

Lead teams through the events, encouraging students to cheer each other on. After all teams have completed all events, gather everyone together for a rest!

impact

For extra

Use this game to spark a discussion about encouragement. Ask:

- *Did you feel encouraged during these activities? Why or why not?*
- *What does the Bible mean when it says to build each other up and encourage each other?*
- *How can you live out those concepts when you play sports or are involved in other forms of competition?*

Junkyard

OVERVIEW: Players will create objects out of assorted pieces of "junk."

TIME INVOLVED: 30 minutes to 2 hours

GROUP SIZE: from 8 to 80 or more participants

SUPPLIES: a large stack of "stuff" from your garage or basement, such as tools, bricks, old toys, plastic jugs and jars, stray nuts and bolts, old magazines, pots and pans, pieces of lumber and cardboard, and broken objects of all sizes and shapes; 10 rubber bands (assorted sizes) and 1 roll of duct tape for each small group of participants

PREPARATION: Gather enough junk so that you have approximately two or three objects for every participant. Create two or three piles of junk in your playing area.

The Game

Once players arrive, have them form small Art Teams of four to six participants.

Say: **I know you all have a secret longing to paint a masterpiece worthy of hanging in the Louvre in Paris, or gracing the elegant halls of the Uffizi Gallery in Florence. You wish to sculpt a magnificent marble figure so powerful and realistic that blood seems to course through its veins.**

In your hearts you are all artists—and today is your day to shine! In your Art Teams, you'll create masterpieces not with paint and stone. Rather, you will transform junk into brilliant art. This calls for *real* talent!

Explain to Art Teams that members of each team will cooperate to create "instant art" sculptures that meet specific goals. Art Teams will have just ten minutes to conceptualize and create their sculptures. Then Art Teams will exhibit their work and explain their subtleties to the larger group.

Have each teenager select one object from each junk pile you've created, then return to his or her Art

LEADER TIP

You determine the scale of this game by choosing small objects out of a "junk drawer" or by hauling in stuff from a junkyard. The smaller the objects, the less space you'll need. If you want to have a full-scale game, take over the church lawn and include mufflers, bumpers, tires, and other auto-related junk. Just be careful about the objects you toss in the junk piles. Watch out for sharp or rusty edges, or you'll be dealing with cut fingers or tetanus shots. Avoid problems by having pairs of work gloves available for students who wish to use them.

Team. Objects collected by the team become the raw materials from which sculptures are created.

After students have collected their objects, explain the following rules. First, let them know that their objects will be used several times, so the sculptures must be created in such a way that they can be easily dismantled. The objects cannot be destroyed, mutilated, or otherwise messed up. Clarify, too, that teams must use *most* of their objects in each sculpture, but do not have to use every single object. Also, the objects may not be used in unsafe ways. Lastly, their sculptures must be sufficiently stable to survive while other Art Teams take turns exhibiting their creations.

Give each Art Team a roll of duct tape and ten assorted rubber bands. They'll use these to hold their sculptures together (hopefully).

Following are five rounds of art assignments. Introduce them one at a time, and allow ten minutes for planning and creation of sculptures, then three minutes per Art Team for explanation and commentary. Allow up to five minutes for dismantling sculptures to prepare for the next round. (If you'd like the game to be shorter, play only one or two rounds.)

ART ASSIGNMENTS:

Round 1: Create a structure that will safely move a mouse from Montana to Moscow.

Round 2: Create a significant work of art that celebrates National Plumbers Week.

Round 3: Design a product that will be featured on the

"Dr. Bernice Diet Dynamos" infomercial. Be able to explain why it works.

Round 4: Create an instrument for the Rock and Roll Museum's display called "The '60s: Music From Unlikely Instruments."

Round 5: Build a prop that will be used in the upcoming feature film *Destruction of Planet Garbanzo.*

impact

for extra

After the game, invite players to gather together and sit in a circle around you. Ask:

- *What was the easiest part of this game? the most difficult part? Why?*
- *If you could be any famous artist, dead or alive, who would you want to be? Why?*
- *How did you feel having to create something from practically nothing? How is that like or unlike your daily life?*
- *Is God artistic? Explain.*

Life Raft

OVERVIEW: Teenagers will work together to transfer their teams and all of their belongings off of a deserted island and onto life rafts.

TIME INVOLVED: 45 minutes to 1 hour 30 minutes

GROUP SIZE: from 14 to 70 or more participants

SUPPLIES: 2 pieces of construction paper per student, 1 can of soda per student, several pairs of scissors, markers, for each team of 7 participants: 1 garbage bag, 2 beach towels, empty 1-gallon milk container, 1 backpack, several hymnals, several paper grocery bags, 1 sleeping bag, 1 bag of oranges, 2 bricks, one 2x4 board, 1 penny

PREPARATION: Select a large grassy outdoor area such as a park. Set up enough "life rafts" so that each team of seven students will have one. The life rafts should form a circle around the central point, each about twenty-five feet from the center (see the diagram below). Each life raft is created by setting two bricks on their long side and setting one 2x4 on these bricks.

Next, create cargo piles for each team in the center area which is the imaginary island. For each team, get two beach towels very wet and put them in a garbage bag, set out a few paper grocery bags, fill the milk carton with water, fill the backpack with hymnals, set out the sleeping bags and the bag of oranges, and set out seven individual cans of pop. Have the construction paper, scissors, and markers ready in a central area.

Game Setup

The Game

When students arrive, invite them to form teams of seven players. First, ask participants to take off their shoes and socks and put them in their team's paper grocery bags. As part of the "island experience," ask the students to remain barefoot throughout the game.

Next, have teams choose a captain, and give each captain a penny. All of the other teammates will become "living bridge" members. Instruct each living bridge member to trace one hand and one foot on pieces of construction paper, cut them out, and then put their initials on one side. Once each team completes all of their hands and feet, they should turn them in to you, the game leader. Be careful to keep each team's handprints and footprints separate.

Now take each group's prints and make a pathway with them from the island to their life raft with the initials on each print facing down. Make sure you put the prints in a random order. Have each team move their cargo (garbage bag, bags of shoes, cans of soda, and so on) to the beginning of their pathway.

> **LEADER TIP**
>
> If it's a windy day, bring along some nails to tack down the handprints and footprints.

Have each team assemble next to its cargo, and welcome all the captains and crews. Tell the students that they are a community that has been stranded on a deserted island. After months of battling the elements, they've decided that it's time to try to sail home, so they're all packing up and setting sail on life rafts. There's only one problem—during a storm, the life rafts were washed out to sea and now are drifting in the ocean. The only way to get all of the people and supplies off the island will be to make a living bridge to the life rafts.

The first step students will take is to build a living bridge to the raft. After they successfully build their bridge, they can start loading cargo onto the raft.

Explain the following game rules to the students. The teams will take turns in a clockwise order. The captain of each team has a penny he or she will flip to determine how many living bridge people can be moved in each turn. If a captain flips the coin and it's "heads," a single living bridge person can move. If the coin turns up "tails," two living bridge teammates can move.

Once a captain knows how many players can move in a particular turn, the captain should pick the living bridge person who he or she believes is represented by the first footprint or handprint on the ground. This chosen person should place his or her foot or hand on the cutout. If it doesn't fit, the team loses its turn, the living bridge member returns to shore, and the next crew takes a turn. However, if it appears to be a match, the captain can instruct the living bridge participant to read out the initials written on the bottom of the construction-paper foot or hand. If they don't match, the living bridge person returns back to the island and the next team begins its turn.

If the choice was correct, the living bridge member should sit down on the spot where his or her foot or handprint lies. If the captain has yet another person to move, the process continues as before. This time, however, the next living bridge person to be chosen must leapfrog over the back of the seated player to get to the next handprint or footprint and check it. If it is a match, that living bridge person can sit down on his or her spot.

This process of coin flipping and selecting living bridge members should continue around the group of crews as they attempt to move off the island.

When a living bridge member's footprint or handprint is repeated, that person must leapfrog over the participants in front of him or her to the next suspected spot in line. Again the checking process takes place to make sure this is the correct living bridge member. If not, the participant simply leapfrogs back to his or her previous place in line and sits back down. If the guess is correct, this person should sit down in his or her new location on the path to the life raft.

When a team successfully completes its living bridge to the life raft, team members should stand up and cheer.

The next step of the game is the loading of cargo. The captain's job is to remain on shore and hand cargo items to the living bridge members who pass the items to the life boat. Living bridge members can *only* stand in the space designated by their own prints. If there are gaps in the line, living bridge members must leapfrog back and forth to their two different spots in order to complete the bridge and pass the objects.

Each team must successfully move a garbage bag filled with wet towels, a gallon of water, a backpack filled with books, seven cans of soda, a bag of oranges, seven sleeping bags, and its bags of shoes onto the raft. The extra challenge here is that not only must they make decisions about dealing with the gaps in their bridge, but they must also each use only one hand to pass objects down the line to the life raft. If an object is dropped, the captain must retrieve it and start it over at the beginning. Once all of the objects are in the rafts, the students can all walk along the pathway to their raft and cheer for the other teams as they finish the challenge.

Ask the students if they have any questions about the directions as you've explained them. Once you've answered any questions, instruct the students to begin the game.

When the game is finished and all of the teams are done, celebrate by inviting them to enjoy the soda and oranges as an island treat!

impact

Use this game to symbolize the teamwork that takes place within the church body. Ask:

- *How have you seen examples of people working together to accomplish the work of ministry at our church?*
- *How can we join in on the work of our church and the ministry to our community?*

Mysterious Mixer

OVERVIEW: Participants attempt to find their teammates by working together to decipher clues they have been given.

TIME INVOLVED: approximately 30 minutes

GROUP SIZE: from 10 to 50 or more participants

SUPPLIES: index cards

PREPARATION: Write items with a theme on each of the index cards. You should choose a uniform number for each category; depending on group size, five or six items per category would be best. Use the lists on p. 93 to help you get started. (Note: Don't write the category anywhere on these cards.) Keep the cards bundled together by category until you know exactly how many students are present. These will be referred to as "clue cards" throughout these directions.

Next, write each of the categories onto separate cards. Make these cards easy to distinguish from clue cards by writing them on colored cards or by using a different colored marker. If needed, create a master list of the categories and their correct clues.

(These categories have six clues.)

Restaurants: Chinese, Italian, Seafood, Mexican, Pizza, Fast-Food

Trees: Walnut, Orange, Pear, Magnolia, Cherry, Pine

Shoes: Bowling, Ballet, Tap, Tennis, Dress, Sandals

Balls: Base, Beach, Foot, Fooz, Soccer, Basket

Fish: Tuna, Sword, Angel, Gold, Cat, Bass

Birds: Blue, Black, Humming, Robin, Cardinal, Sparrow

Bands: Rock, Rubber, Head, Sweat, Wrist, Waist

Teeth: Wisdom, Incisors, Molars, Baby, Permanent, Dentures

Hats and Caps: Top, Straw, Chef, Sailor, Baseball, Stocking

(These categories have five clues.)

Bags: Trash, Lawn, Duffle, Overnight, Garbage

Candy: Cotton, Chocolate, Hard, Caramel, Licorice

Light: Black, Flash, Christmas, Neon, Sun

Flakes: Corn, Bran, Frosted, Snow, Dandruff

Tapes: Video, Cassette, Masking, Transparent, Duct

Parks: Theme, State, Water, Amusement, Roadside

Storms: Thunder, Tropical, Electrical, Wind, Hurricane

(These categories have four clues.)

Brushes: Hair, Tooth, Toilet, Nail

Tables: Coffee, End, Dining Room, Picnic

Bees: Bumble, Honey, Spelling, Killer

The Game

When teenagers arrive, explain that teams will be given a category and then will search for hiding students who have clue cards that fit within their team's given category. Read one of the above lists as an example.

Distribute clue cards to a little more than half of the students. Participants should not show these cards to anyone until the game has begun. Remember, each category must have an equal number of clue cards and teams should know exactly how many clue cards fit within the categories.

Explain to the teenagers with clue cards that they should hide and when a group finds them, they should present their card. If that group believes the particular clue card matches the team's category, the hiding teenager will join that group and help them search for others. Hiding players should stay in the same location until a group has selected them. Give these players several minutes to hide all over the building or playing field before sending out the remaining players.

Assign the remaining teenagers to teams, and give each team a category card. Make sure the categories you hand out match the clues previously given to the hiding teenagers. Remind these groups that their teammates are hiding all over the playing field. They must search to find them. When they find a hiding player, they will be shown a clue card. If this clue matches their assigned category, that teenager will join the group and help in the search for the remaining clues. Designate a meeting place where teams should go when they have found all of their players.

LEADER TIP

For more of a challenge, or for confined indoor play, make these modifications. Omit the category cards. Give all participants clue cards. Read a sample list, and explain that they should try to find their teammates by finding the clues that have something in common with the clue they have been given. Participants should try to form teams and figure out what their particular category is.

Give hints as the game progresses using your master list. For example, after five or ten minutes, read two clues from each list to help students make a match. After five additional minutes, give each pair another clue from their category. Continue until all students have found their groups. Then, invite them to reveal their categories to the other groups.

impact

For extra...

When the game has ended, say: *You are reaching an age in life when you have to make all kinds of decisions about your future in a short amount of time. This process can feel a little like this game as you search for clues or pieces to a puzzle that will tell you what you're supposed to do or be. It's so important to rely on God at this time in your life and pray for his guidance. Unlike us, he knows the future just as if it happened yesterday!*

Invite a volunteer to read Proverbs 3:5-7 aloud. Ask:
* *Can you describe a time when you had to rely on God instead of doing what seemed logical to you or others?*
* *How does God guide us?*
* *What makes it difficult to trust God with the future?*
* *What are some specific ways that you can rely on God more?*

Mystery Design Workshop

OVERVIEW: Students will work together in teams to design Legos creations inside of garbage bags.

TIME INVOLVED: 30 to 45 minutes

GROUP SIZE: from 4 to 64 or more participants

SUPPLIES: several hundred Lego plastic construction toys, large black garbage bags, garbage bag ties, newsprint, pencils

PREPARATION: Determine the number of teams you'll have (two to eight students per team), and fill that number of garbage bags with an equal number of Legos, tying off the bags at the top.

The Game

After students arrive, have them form equal teams of two to eight students. Invite each team to pick up a garbage bag, pencils, and a large piece of newsprint. Prompt teams to spread out around your meeting room, and tell them that they cannot, under any circumstances, open their garbage bags or tear holes in them.

Once teams are settled, inform them that their bags are filled with all the necessary elements they'll need to design and build fantastic creations. Each team's job will be to design, on paper, a blueprint of what the team will create with the Legos inside of the bag. After team members decide on a design, they will work together to build their creation using every single Lego piece in the bag.

What's the hitch? Students must accomplish their design construction without opening their black bags. They must build their creations *inside the bags*—in other words, they must manipulate and assemble the building materials through the plastic sides of the garbage bags. They won't be able to see their creations—they'll have to use only their hands to feel what their creations "look like" through the plastic bag.

Give teams five to ten minutes to feel what is inside of their bags, decide what they'd like to build, and draw their blueprints. Once they've drawn their blueprints, collect all of the pencils.

> **LEADER TIP**
> If students have a hard time deciding what to create, you may want to offer the following suggestions: a house, a castle, a boat, a car, an animal, or a person.

Allow students fifteen to thirty minutes to work together to construct their designs. Once all of the teams have finished building their designs, gather all of the students back together for an unveiling of their creations.

Have a member of one of the groups display his or her team's blueprint for the other students and explain what the team set out to build. Then have the team work together to gently open the bag and reveal what's inside. Students may be surprised by their accuracy or their error!

LEADER TIP

You may want to give each team a special award for their mystery design. Some possibilities are Most Difficult Design, Most Creative Effort, Most Interesting Color Scheme, or Most Accurate Construction.

Invite each team to follow the first, displaying its blueprint and then revealing its creation. After each team presents its design, lead the rest of the students in a round of applause congratulating that team's ingenuity and hard work.

impact

For extra

Use this game to lead students in a discussion of how our plans in life don't always work out as we hope. Ask:
- *What types of "blueprints" do you have for your own life? for your future?*
- *Do you ever feel like you're making decisions or building your future in the dark?*
- *How can God help you as you plan for your future?*

Ninja Bob

OVERVIEW: The virtuous Ninja Bob will work to secretly "convert" all of the other students to become his followers without being caught.

TIME INVOLVED: 20 to 30 minutes

GROUP SIZE: from 20 to 60 or more participants

SUPPLIES: jellybeans (one should be black), bowl, several basketballs, volleyballs, Frisbee discs, soccer balls

PREPARATION: Before you begin the game, count out one jellybean for each student and put them all in a bowl. Make sure that one, and *only* one, of the jellybeans in the bowl is black.

The Game

When students arrive, welcome them to the game and take a few minutes to explain the plot of the game by telling them the story of the mysterious Ninja Bob. Explain that legend tells of an amazing ninja named Bob who was the greatest martial arts master of the land. However, an evil martial arts master came on the scene, beat Ninja Bob in a fight, and vanquished Ninja Bob from his dojo. The evil master took over Ninja Bob's dojo and brainwashed all of Ninja Bob's followers, turning them into his own students. Since then, no one has seen or heard from Ninja Bob.

Explain that rumor has it that Ninja Bob has secretly returned and is trying to reclaim his old dojo and convert his former students into his own followers again.

Tell the students that in the game you will be the evil martial arts master and all of the students are your brainwashed followers. One of them will secretly be chosen as Ninja Bob, and that student's job will be to convert all of the other students to become his own followers once again.

To convert a student, Ninja Bob only needs to tap him or her on the shoulder three consecutive times. The student who is tapped on the shoulder by Ninja Bob must then respond by signaling back with a tap on the top of his or her head. Once this sequence is completed, the student has been converted into a follower of Ninja Bob and will join Ninja Bob in the job of converting the other students by tapping others on the shoulder three times. Once converted, Ninja Bob's new followers should keep their conversion a secret so that they can easily blend in with the other brainwashed students in the dojo.

All of these actions should be done in complete secrecy so that Ninja Bob and his followers are not caught by the other players. If any of the unconverted students thinks he or she has seen Ninja Bob or one of his followers trying to convert another student, he or she should take that person to you, the evil martial arts master. If the student is Ninja Bob, then the game is over and Ninja Bob has failed in his or her effort to reclaim his dojo. If the student is one of Ninja Bob's followers, he or she must sit out the rest of the game. If the accused player is *not* a follower of Ninja Bob, the accusing student must sit out the rest of the game.

If Ninja Bob and his followers are able to convert all of the other students, the game is won.

Invite the students to take a jellybean from the bowl one at a time and look at its color, then eat it. Make sure teenagers give each other space so that no one else sees the color of the jellybean each player draws. Announce that whoever had the

LEADER TIP

If Ninja Bob is caught early in the game, start the game over with a new secret Ninja Bob. This game can be repeated as often as you'd like!

black jellybean is now Ninja Bob and has the job of covertly converting the other students to become his followers.

As the evil martial arts master, you demand that your students continuously train and hone their skills. All of the students need to be participating in different types of athletic training constantly throughout the entire game. Point out the basketballs, soccer balls, Frisbee discs, and volleyballs, and instruct the students to play together, running drills and every so often switching to one of the other sports.

After you've explained all of these rules, ask the students if they have any questions. Once you've answered any questions, begin the game!

impact

For extra

Use this game to kick off a discussion about sharing faith. Ask:

- *How were Ninja Bob's efforts similar to someone working to share his or her faith in Christ? How were they different?*
- *Have you ever felt like you had to "hide" your faith like Ninja Bob hid his identity?*
- *Is it ever OK to hide your faith? Why or why not?*
- *In this game, a large number of people were "converted" to become Ninja Bob's followers in a short amount of time. How can sharing faith spread from person to person in a similar way?*
- *How can we encourage each other in our efforts to share our faith in Jesus with others?*

Past·Present·Future Shuffle

OVERVIEW: Players will work in teams to identify mysterious wrapped objects and then guess who the objects' owners are.

TIME INVOLVED: 30 minutes to 1 hour

GROUP SIZE: from 16 to 40 or more participants

Supplies: index cards, envelopes, table, pens

Preparation: About one week prior to the game, give each student an index card and an envelope. Each student should write on his or her card either a valuable memory from the past, something he or she highly values in the present, or a goal for the future. Students should indicate on the top of the cards if they wrote about their past, present, or future.

Their job throughout the week will be for each student to find an object that in some way symbolizes what he or she wrote down on the card. For example, if someone's past memory is going to the zoo with his or her grandmother as a young child, the student could select a stuffed animal such as a zebra. Or, if someone's future goal is to become a fashion designer, he or she could select a swatch of fabric.

Once they select their objects, students should wrap them in wrapping paper (or newspaper, grocery bag paper, or whatever). It's important that they not put them in a box first—the objects need to be wrapped as they are so that others will be able to guess what they are. Students should then write what the objects are on the index cards that they wrote on earlier and stick the cards in their envelopes. Students should tape their envelopes to the bottom of their wrapped objects.

The Game

When students arrive, have them secretly deposit their wrapped objects in another room so that no one else can see which objects they brought. Once all of the objects have been dropped off, bring them into the meeting area and display them on a table, side by side.

Have students break into groups of four, and assign a number to each group. Explain that their job will be to work in their groups to identify what the wrapped objects are and to correctly guess who brought the object as well as what the object means to that person. By correctly guessing an object and the person who brought it, the group gains that person as a team member. The goal of the game is to get as many other students as possible on their teams.

Give students a few minutes to talk in their groups, secretly sharing which objects each of them brought, but keeping the meanings secret. Then let the guessing begin! Groups can walk around the table, examining the wrapped objects, picking them up, and so on. When a group decides unanimously that they'd like to guess on the identity of a wrapped object, they simply need to approach you, the game leader, and make their guess. (Groups are *not* allowed to guess on the identity of any of the objects their own group members brought.)

To check if they've guessed correctly, you'll open the envelope on the bottom of the object and look to see if they are right. If they're wrong, they can take only two more guesses on that particular object throughout the game. If all three of the guesses are incorrect, they can no longer guess on that object and must only guess on other objects.

If a group guesses correctly, they can unwrap the object and set it back on the table. You'll write their group number on the envelope and set it in front of the object on the table.

Once a group has guessed an object correctly, they can now begin trying to guess who brought the object and what it represents. Only the group who correctly identified the object is allowed to question people about it—none of the other groups can guess about that object.

The group must decide, though, if they'd like to keep on trying to identify the other objects (which they have to do unanimously) or if they'd like to work on tracking down the object's owner. Groups may split up and ask questions while one member of the group works on identifying the objects, but that group member cannot make any guesses until he or she has gotten the full verbal agreement of each group member for each specific guess.

In their effort to identify the objects' owners, group members can split up or work together, asking the other students yes or no questions. If a student is being questioned, he or she must stop whatever he or she is doing and honestly answer all of the questions being posed to him or her. Questions can be very direct, such as "Did you bring the zebra?" or "Does it represent a goal for your future?" The more difficult task will be trying to uncover why the person brought that object. Some good questions to discover the meanings of the objects may be "Does this have to do with one of your hobbies?" or "Does this memory involve other family members?"

If someone guesses another student's object and reason, the guessed student now must leave the team he or she was on and join the team that correctly guessed his or her object and meaning. The guessed student must notify each of his or her old team members that the student is leaving the group to join another group. The guessed student is now permanently part of the new team and cannot be guessed by any other teams. To indicate this change in group status, the guessed student should go to the table, take the index card out of his or her object's envelope, and write his or her name and new team number on it. The guessed team member should now be loyal to his or her new team and can feel free to share what the objects are that his or her original team members brought.

Groups will work like this, guessing what the wrapped objects are and then trying to track down the objects' owners, simultaneously—and as various students' objects and meanings are guessed, they'll shuffle from team to team. Pretty soon, the original numbered groups will be filled with different students and some groups may completely disappear as all four members join other teams.

> **LEADER TIP**
>
> If one (or a few) of the objects has not been identified and the game is coming to a standstill, announce that each team gets three more guesses about that particular object. Likewise, if it appears that many of the objects have been identified, but teams are having a difficult time guessing the meanings for the various objects, announce that all of the students being questioned must give one obvious hint to their questioner to help the guessing process along.

The game ends when all of the objects and owners have been correctly guessed. Congratulate the students on their teamwork and their efforts to get to know each other better.

for extra impact

After the game, gather the students together. Ask:

- *What are some new things you learned about each other?*
- *How can our past memories, present values, or future goals tell others more about us?*
- *How can learning new things about others improve your relationships?*

Pudding Cup

OVERVIEW: Students will create silly poetry by linking up with other students.

TIME INVOLVED: 20 to 30 minutes

GROUP SIZE: from 10 to 100 or more participants

SUPPLIES: photocopy of "Word List" (pp. 103-104), hat or bowl

PREPARATION: Photocopy the "Word List" (pp. 103-104), and cut apart the words. Use the chart below to determine how many of each word category you should place in the hat or bowl.

If you have this many **players...**	Use this many **pronouns**	Use this many **connecting words**	Use this many **verbs**	Use this many **adverbs and adjectives**	Use this many **nouns**
10 to 20	3	3	4	5	5
21 to 40	5	8	8	11	8
41 to 60	5	12	12	18	13
61 to 80	5	17	18	22	18
81 or more	All of them	All of them	All of them	All of them	All of them

The Game

Begin by having participants each draw a word from the hat or bowl. Explain that the object of this game is for each student to connect with other students to create phrases and, eventually, silly poetry.

In order to do this, each player may say *only* the word on his or her paper and nothing else. Students may use hand motions and change the tone of their voice in an effort to communicate, but they must remain limited to a singular vocabulary. Once they find another word to connect with, students should join hands and walk around together. Once several phrases have been formed, players should try to organize themselves into a unique poem.

Explain that students *can* change the tense of their word depending on their situation, but they may not change the word entirely. For example "do" can be changed to "did" or "does" if needed.

Clarify that this game is not a competition or race—it's just to have fun and showcase the group's creativity. Play several rounds!

word list

LIST ONE: Pronouns	He	I	She	They	We
LIST TWO: Connecting Words	A	About	Am	Among	And
	At	Be	Beneath	Between	But
	Can	Could	In	Into	May
	Might	Must	Not	Off	On
	Or	The	Though	Will	With
LIST THREE: Verbs	Blend	Build	Carry	Chew	Would
	Clean	Cram	Create	Crush	Dance
	Dip	Download	Draw	Dream	Drive
	Dunk	Elaborate	Elude	Enjoy	Experience
	Fall	Fish	Fling	Fly	Glow
	Grow	Gyrate	Hang	Hate	Help
	Hide	Hit	Hitch	Hold	Hope
	Hover	Hurt	Jingle	Jump	Kiss
	Lean	Love	Lower	Mingle	Mix
	Motion	Move	Munch	Paint	Plop
	Plow	Preach	Pull	Push	Shout
	Shove	Sing	Swim	Whisper	
LIST FOUR: Adverbs and Adjectives	Angelic	Angrily	Bouncy	Boyish	Broken
	Devilish	Fat-Free	Forcefully	Frivolous	Frosted

LIST FOUR: Adverbs and Adjectives, cont.	Frozen	Gigantic	Girlie	Gravitationally	Gulp
	Gurgle	Hairy	Hand-carved	Happy	Haunting
	Honest	Hot	Huge	Infuriatingly	Intelligent
	Jealous	Jovial	Kindly	Lanky	Late
	Long	Loopy	Loudly	Lovely	Lucky
	Lumbering	Maggot-infested	Magic	Microscopic	Mud-caked
	Peacefully	Persnickety	Quiet	Rose-colored	Rotting
	Sheepish	Slow-moving	Sluggish	Softly	Stylish
	Superfluous	Sweat-covered	Teal	Terrific	Tiny
	Unceremoniously	Unknowingly	Unmentionable		
LIST FIVE: Nouns	Book	Boyfriend	Brain Freeze	Canned Fruit	CD Player
	Cheese	Donkey	Door Handle	Footrest	Girlfriend
	Golf Cart	Goober	Head	Honey	Iron
	Knife	Language	Lather	Letter	Lie
	Life	Light	Liver	Lung	Megaphone
	Mercedes Benz	Moon Phase	Mosh Pit	Movie Theater	Mummy's Tomb
	Nana	Noodle	Ocean Liner	Pet Lizard	Poem
	Poodle	Pudding Cup	Rotary Engine	Rubber Chicken	Saliva
	Soap Bubble	Soda Spray	Song	Spleen	Stone
	Toenail	Trombone	Watch Fob	Watermelon	

For extra impact

Use this game to discuss the relationship between speech and faith. Ask:
- *What is your favorite word of all time? What is your least favorite word?*
- *What word do you think causes the most damage to another person? What word has hurt you the most?*

Conclude by inviting a student to read Luke 6:45 and Colossians 4:6 aloud.

What's Up?

OVERVIEW: Participants, speaking only in code, will try to identify other team members who are speaking the same code.

TIME INVOLVED: 15 minutes to 1 hour (depending on group size)

GROUP SIZE: from 12 to 60 or more participants

SUPPLIES: photocopies of "Crazy Code-Talkin' Instructions" (p. 107), envelopes

PREPARATION: Make photocopies of the "Crazy Code-Talkin' Instructions" handout on p. 107, and cut them into slips. Make enough copies so that each student will get one slip. Put each of the slips in an envelope.

The Game

When students arrive, tell them that they're each going to receive a secret code that they'll use to communicate. Their goal will be to identify all of the other students in the group who are speaking the same code.

Explain that all of them will use the same format to have conversations with each other. First they'll ask "What's up?" then they'll supply a code word and say it is "what's up." Finally, they'll supply a decoy word (not part of the code) and say it is *not* "what's up."

Demonstrate a few examples for them with a code that only uses five-letter words. Say: **What's up? Pizza is what's up! Sandwiches are not what's up. What's up? Music is what's up! Silence is not what's up. What's up? Black is what's up! Yellow is not what's up. What's up? A snake is what's up! A fish is not what's up.**

After you've demonstrated the What's-Up pattern of conversation, ask if students have any questions about what you've just explained. Once you've answered their questions, let them know that when the game begins, they'll only be able to speak using this pattern of conversation as they talk to each other.

Now pass out an envelope to each student, and ask them all to go somewhere in the room where they can privately open their envelopes and read their code instructions, being careful not to reveal the contents of their envelopes to anyone. Let them know that if they don't understand their code instructions, they can whisper any questions to you and you'll try to explain it. After a few minutes for reading their code instructions, have the students come back together.

Explain that once students start talking in their codes, their goal is to find and identify other students who are speaking the same code. During a What's-Up? conversation with another student, if a player thinks the person is speaking the same code, he or she should wink at the other student. If the other person also thinks they're speaking the same code, the student should wink back. When stu-

dents identify other members of their Code-Talkin' group, they should start traveling around the room together.

However, if one of the students isn't sure that his or her conversation partner is speaking the same code, he or she should shrug his or her shoulders. If one of the students is certain that the other player is *not* speaking the same code, he or she should shake his or her head and move on to a conversation with someone else.

Invite the students to randomly form groups of five or six students, and let them know that when you start the game, they'll have four minutes to mingle in their groups, only talking their codes. When the four minutes are up, you'll let everyone know that they are free to mingle all about the room, speaking in What's Up conversation to each other.

crazy code·talkin' instructions

Your Code: Same beginnings and endings

Use only words that begin and end with the same letter.

Examples: willow, dead, gang, tent, noon

---

crazy code·talkin' instructions

Your Code: Ha-Ha! words

Use only pairs of words that both begin with the letters "ha."

Examples: halo hat, harmful hamster, harmonica habitat, hazardous hankies, happy hallelujahs

---

crazy code·talkin' instructions

Your Code: Six-letter words

Use only words that contain six letters.

Examples: bridge, paints, planet, skates, orange

---

crazy code·talkin' instructions

Your Code: Oo-words

Use only words with an "oo" sound.

Examples: moo, fruit, cool, shoe, new

---

crazy code·talkin' instructions

Your Code: ABCs

Use only words that begin with A, B, or C.

Examples: Alabama, amazing, ballet, burger, cat

---

crazy code·talkin' instructions

Your Code: Three-letter words

Use only words that have three letters.

Examples: cap, ice, eye, now, nap

If students don't have any more questions, begin the game!

Once it appears that all (or most) of the students have identified their other Code-Talkin' group members, call an end to the game, and let the students know that they can now break the code and talk normally. Invite them to share with the others in their group what code they were speaking and verify if they identified the other code talkers correctly. If some of the students are in the wrong groups, have them find the right group and join them.

End by inviting Code-Talkin' groups to reveal their codes to each other and congratulating the students on a job well done.

For extra impact

Use this game to get your students thinking about the challenges of communicating with others, especially when it comes to talking about faith. Ask:

- *How was speaking different codes in this game similar to the different ways people talk about God, faith, or spirituality?*
- *What are some examples of "code words" Christians use that other people may not understand?*
- *How can we better communicate these ideas?*
- *What are some keys to overcoming communication challenges with people who may not understand where we're coming from?*

Word-O Hoops

OVERVIEW: Students will work together to create words using tennis balls.

TIME INVOLVED: 10 to 30 minutes

GROUP SIZE: from 8 to 40 participants

SUPPLIES: 5 plastic hoops, tennis balls (a minimum of 26; if you have more than 13 players, you'll need at least 2 tennis balls per player), permanent marker

PREPARATION: Legibly print each of the letters of the alphabet on a tennis ball. If you have more than twenty-six tennis balls, continue writing out the alphabet until you've used up all the tennis balls. (Or, write some more commonly used letters in the alphabet on the extra tennis balls, such as A, E, I, L, N, O, P, R, S, or T.) Place one plastic hoop in the center of your playing area, and put all of the tennis balls inside it. Place each of the other four hoops in one of the corners of your playing area.

The Game

Have students form four equal-sized groups, and have each group choose one of the corner hoops as their own. Point out the lettered tennis balls in the center hoop, and explain that each group's goal is to find the letters they need to spell a word in their hoop. They can spell any word they'd like as long as it has a minimum of five letters (and can be repeated in front of their mothers).

To begin play, one person from each corner group will race to the center hoop, grab a tennis ball, and run back to his or her team, dropping the ball in their hoop. As soon as their ball is settled inside the hoop (and not bouncing around the floor), another person from that team can race to get another ball. Here's where it gets crazy: That player can either run to the center hoop to get a letter *or* can grab a ball from another team's hoop.

> **LEADER TIP**
>
> It's up to you to set parameters for the types of words you'll accept. Make sure to clarify with students if you'll accept proper nouns (names of people, places, and so on) or slang words. You may want to bring a dictionary just to be on the safe side!

This relay process continues as teams try to fill their hoops with enough letters to spell a five-letter (or more) word. When a team thinks they've formed a word, the entire team needs to jump up and shout "Word-O!" When a team yells "Word-O!" all teams need to freeze while you check to see if the team has actually spelled a word. If they were successful, lead all the groups in a round of applause, and then start the game over again.

impact

For extra

After several rounds of play, have teams discuss the following questions. Ask:
- *What skills did you need to have in order to play this game well?*
- *Did some of the members of your group have different skills?*
- *How would this game have gone if everyone was good at only one part of the game?*
- *Why is it important to understand and utilize everyone's unique gifts?*

over·the·top games for youth ministry

indexes

Discussion Theme Index

Scripture Index

Group Size Index

SMALL GROUPS

(approximately twenty or fewer participants)

MEDIUM GROUPS

(approximately twenty to fifty participants)

LARGE GROUPS

(approximately fifty or more participants)

Any Size

Setting Index

Indoor Games

Outside Games

Flexible Setting Games

Time Involved Index

Short Games
(approximately thirty minutes or less)

Medium Games
(approximately thirty minutes to one hour)

Long Games
(one hour or more)